PERT MATH PRACTICE TESTS
Florida Postsecondary Education Readiness Test
Math Preparation Study Guide
with 250 Problems and Solutions

PERT and the Postsecondary Educational Readiness Test are trademarks of McCann Testing. Neither McCann Testing nor the Florida Department of Education are affiliated with or endorse this publication.

PERT Math Practice Tests: Florida Postsecondary Education Readiness Test Math Preparation Study Guide with 400 Problems and Solutions

© COPYRIGHT 2018 by Exam SAM Study Aids & Media

All rights reserved. No part of this publication may be reproduced, stored in a retrieval system, or transmitted, in any form or by any means, electronic, mechanical, photocopying, recording, or otherwise, without the prior written permission of the copyright owner.

ISBN-13: 978-0-9998087-8-8
ISBN-10: 0-9998087-8-8

For information on bulk discounts, please contact us at: email@examsam.com

The drawings in this publication are for illustration purposes only. They are not drawn to an exact scale.

PERT and the Postsecondary Educational Readiness Test are trademarks of McCann Testing. Neither McCann Testing nor the Florida Department of Education are affiliated with or endorse this publication.

TABLE OF CONTENTS

How to Use this Publication   i

PERT Math Practice Test Set 1 – Questions 1 to 50:

Applying Standard Concepts

    Basic Computations with Integers   1

    Multiplying Fractions   1

    Dividing Fractions   1

    Adding Fractions   2

    Lowest Common Denominator   2

    Simplifying Fractions   2

    Subtracting Fractions   2

    Order of Operations (PEMDAS)   3

    Improper Fractions   3

    Percentages   3

    Working with Prices and Profits   4

    Decimals and Decimal Places   4

    Remainders   4

    Operations on Decimal Numbers   4

    Ordering Numbers   5

    Practical Problems   5

    Greatest and Fewest Multiples   6

Algebra

Roots and Radicals 7

Exponent Laws 8

Simplifying Rational Algebraic Expressions 9

Factoring Polynomials 10

Expanding Polynomials 10

Linear Equations 11

Algebraic and Polynomial Functions 12

Quadratic Equations 13

Linear Inequalities 14

Quadratic Inequalities 14

Systems of Equations 14

Coordinate Geometry

Midpoint formula 15

Distance formula 15

Slope and slope-intercept 15

x and y intercepts 16

PERT Math Practice Questions 51 to 250:

PERT Math Practice Test Set 2 – Questions 51 to 100 17

PERT Math Practice Test Set 3 – Questions 101 to 150 27

PERT Math Practice Test Set 4 – Questions 151 to 200 37

PERT Math Practice Test Set 5 – Questions 201 to 250 47

Solutions and Explanations to Questions 1 to 250:

    Solutions and Explanations for Practice Test Set 1 – Questions 1 to 50   57

    Solutions and Explanations for Practice Test Set 2 – Questions 51 to 100   70

    Solutions and Explanations for Practice Test Set 3 – Questions 101 to 150   83

    Solutions and Explanations for Practice Test Set 4 – Questions 151 to 200   96

    Solutions and Explanations for Practice Test Set 5 – Questions 201 to 250   109

Answer Key to All Questions   121

HOW TO USE THIS PUBLICATION

The PERT math exam has problems on algebra and applying standard concepts.

You will find the problems in this study guide a bit easier to complete if you have knowledge of basic arithmetic operations, such as addition, subtraction, multiplication, and division.

You may feel that you need to review arithmetic and elementary algebra before you try the practice problems in this book.

If so, you should try our free practice exercises in arithmetic and elementary algebra first.

The free review problems can be found at: www.examsam.com

As you work through this study guide, you will notice that practice test questions 1 to 50 provide study tips after each question.

The format of the first set of practice test questions introduces all of the concepts on the exam. This will help you learn the strategies and formulas that you need to answer all of the types of questions on the actual examination.

You can refer back to the formulas and tips introduced in part 1 as you work through the remaining material in the book.

Ideally, you should try to memorize the formulas and tips before you complete the remaining practice test questions in the book.

The solutions and explanations for all of the questions are provided after the 400th question.

The answer key is provided at the end of the book.

PERT Math Practice Test Set 1 – Questions 1 to 50:

Applying Standard Concepts

1) − (−6) + 2 = ?
   A) −8
   B) −4
   C) 4
   D) 8

> Computations with signed numbers are frequently included on the examination. Many of these types of problems will involve integers. Integers are positive and negative whole numbers. Integers cannot have decimals, nor can they be mixed numbers. In other words, they can't contain fractions. One of the most important concepts to remember when working with signed numbers is that two negative signs together make a positive number. So, when you see a number like − (−2) you have to use 2 in your calculation.

2) What is the largest possible product of two even integers whose sum is 30?
   A) 14
   B) 16
   C) 210
   D) 224

> You will also see problems that ask you to perform multiplication or division on integers. Some of these problems may ask you to find an integer that meets certain mathematical requirements, like the problem above.

3) $\frac{1}{5} \times \frac{2}{3} = ?$
   A) $\frac{1}{4}$
   B) $\frac{3}{8}$
   C) $\frac{2}{15}$
   D) $\frac{10}{3}$

> You will see problems on the exam that ask you to multiply fractions. To multiply fractions, you first need to multiply the numerators from each fraction. Then multiply the denominators. The numerator is the number on the top of each fraction. The denominator is the number on the bottom of the fraction.

4) $\frac{4}{7} \div \frac{2}{3} = ?$
   A) $\frac{8}{21}$
   B) $\frac{12}{14}$
   C) $\frac{6}{8}$
   D) $\frac{14}{12}$

You will also need to know how to divide fractions for the exam. To divide fractions, invert the second fraction by putting the denominator on the top and numerator on the bottom. Then multiply as indicated for the previous problem.

5) $\frac{1}{8} + \frac{3}{16} = ?$

   A) $\frac{5}{16}$

   B) $\frac{4}{24}$

   C) $\frac{16}{5}$

   D) $\frac{24}{16}$

In some fraction problems, you will have to find the lowest common denominator. In other words, before you add or subtract fractions, you have to change them so that the bottom numbers in each fraction are the same. You do this by multiplying the numerator by the same number that you used when multiplying to get the new denominator for the fraction.

6) Simplify: $\frac{12}{14}$

   A) $\frac{1}{7}$

   B) $\frac{4}{7}$

   C) $\frac{7}{6}$

   D) $\frac{6}{7}$

You will also need to know how to simplify fractions for your exam. To simplify fractions, look to see what factors are common to both the numerator and denominator. Factoring is like taking a number apart. So, what numbers can we multiply together to get 12? What numbers can we multiply together to get 14?

7) $4\frac{1}{8} - 3\frac{5}{6} = ?$

   A) $-1\frac{1}{2}$

   B) $1\frac{17}{24}$

   C) $\frac{7}{24}$

   D) $\frac{24}{7}$

> Mixed numbers are those that contain a whole number and a fraction. Convert the mixed numbers back to fractions first. Then find the lowest common denominator of the fractions in order to solve the problem.

8) $-5 \times 4 - 6 \div 3 = ?$

   A) -22

   B) $-\dfrac{26}{3}$

   C) -18

   D) $\dfrac{10}{3}$

9) Express as an improper fraction: $\dfrac{4 \times (5-2)^3 + 6}{7 - 4 \div 2}$

   A) $\dfrac{60}{5}$

   B) $\dfrac{114}{5}$

   C) $\dfrac{114}{1.5}$

   D) $\dfrac{60}{1.5}$

> These two questions test your knowledge of order of operations. The phrase "order of operations" means that you need to know which mathematical operation to do first when you are faced with longer problems. Remember the acronym PEMDAS. "PEMDAS" means that you have to do the mathematical operations in this order: First: Do operations inside **P**arentheses; Second: Do operations with **E**xponents; Third: Do **M**ultiplication and **D**ivision (from left to right); Last: Do **A**ddition and **S**ubtraction (from left to right)

10) The price of a certain book is reduced from $60 to $45 at the end of the semester. By what percent is the price of the book reduced?
    A) 15%
    B) 20%
    C) 25%
    D) 33%

> You will have to calculate percentages and decimals on the exam, as well as use percentages and decimals to solve other types of math problems or to create equations. Percentages can be expressed by using the symbol %. They can also be expressed as fractions or decimals. This particular question asks you to perform a calculation in order to determine the percentage discount on an item. Calculate the dollar amount of the reduction by subtracting the sales price from the original price. Then divide the dollar value of the reduction by the original price to get the percentage.

11) A company buys an item at a cost of B and sells it at five times the cost. Which of the following represents the profit made on each item?
   A) B
   B) 4B
   C) 5B
   D) 5 − B

You will see questions on the test that ask you solve real-life problems from basic information. Read the problem carefully and then decide which arithmetic operations are needed in order to solve it. The problem tells us that cell phones sell for four times the cost, so "four times" means that we have to multiply. For this problem, profit is calculated by taking the sales price and subtracting the cost.

12) What is 0.96547 rounded to the nearest thousandth?
   A) 0.96
   B) 0.97
   C) 0.966
   D) 0.965

13) When 1523.48 is divided by 100, which digit of the resulting number is in the tenths place?
   A) 1
   B) 2
   C) 3
   D) 4

These two questions assess your understanding of decimals. Remember that the number after the decimal is in the tenths place, the second number after the decimal is in the hundredths place, and the third number after the decimal is in the thousandths place.

14) What is the remainder when 11 is divided by 3?
   A) 0.66
   B) 0.67
   C) 2
   D) 3

The remainder is the amount that is left over after you divide into whole numbers. These whole numbers are referred to as factors. So, ask yourself what products can be calculated by multiplying another number by 3: 1 × 3 = 3; 2 × 3 = 6; 3 × 3 = 9; 4 × 3 = 12 and so on.

15) 4.25 + 0.003 + 0.148 = ?
   A) 4.401
   B) 4.428
   C) 5.76
   D) 44.01

Line up the decimal points when you add up and remember to carry the 1 where needed.

16) The numbers in the following list are ordered from greatest to least: Θ , η , $^{25}/_{13}$, $^{10}/_9$, $^{1}/_3$
Which of the following could be the value of η?
A) $\sqrt{36}$
B) $^{25}/_{14}$
C) $^{24}/_{13}$
D) 1.91

This problem is asking you to determine missing values from an ordered list of fractions and other numbers. You may find it easier to solve problems like this one if you convert the fractions to decimals.

17) If $7x$ is between 5 and 6, which of the following could be the value of x?
A) $^2/_3$
B) $^3/_4$
C) $^5/_8$
D) $^7/_8$

To solve the problem, set up an inequality as follows: $5 < 7x < 6$. Then put the fractions from the answer choices in for x in order to solve the problem. When a problem asks you to multiply a whole number by a fraction, multiply the whole number by the numerator and then divide this result by the denominator.

18) The temperature on Saturday was 62° F at 5:00 PM and 38° F at 11:00 PM. If the temperature fell at a constant rate on Saturday, what was the temperature at 9:00 PM?
A) 58° F
B) 54° F
C) 50° F
D) 46° F

This question assesses your knowledge of performing operations on integers. Here, we have to perform the operations of subtraction, multiplication, and division.

19) A painter needs to paint 8 rooms, each of which have a surface area of 2000 square feet. If one bucket of paint covers 900 square feet, what is the fewest number of buckets of paint that must be used to complete all 8 rooms?
A) 3
B) 17
C) 18
D) 19

This is a question that requires you to find the fewest multiples of an item. Be mindful of the words "fewest" and "greatest" in problems like this one, since it will normally be impossible to purchase a fractional part of the item in the question. Therefore, you will need to round your result up or down to the nearest whole number accordingly.

20) Soon Li jogged 3.6 miles in ³/₄ of an hour. What was her average jogging speed in miles per hour?
   A) 2.7
   B) 4.0
   C) 4.2
   D) 4.8

This problem involves the calculation of miles per hour with fractional parts of hours. To solve the problem, divide the distance traveled by the time in order to get the speed in miles per hour.

21) A club has 25 members. If each member pays $15 in annual fees, how much money will the club collect in total for the membership fees?
   A) $375
   B) $355
   C) $325
   D) $295

22) A farmer has a field in which cows craze. He is going to buy fence panels to put up a fence along one side of the field. Each panel is 8 feet 6 inches long. He needs 11 panels to cover the entire side of the field. How long is the field?
   A) 60 feet 6 inches
   B) 72 feet 8 inches
   C) 93 feet 6 inches
   D) 102 feet 8 inches

These two problems are asking you to calculate the total amount of a multiple of an item. You therefore need to multiply to solve.

23) Which of the following is the greatest?
   A) 0.350
   B) 0.035
   C) 0.053
   D) 0.3035

For problems asking you to decide which decimal number is the greatest, place all of the numbers in a column with the decimal pints lined up. Then compare the numbers.

Algebra

Roots and Radicals

24) Which of the answers below is equal to the following radical expression? $\sqrt{50}$
   A) $1 \div 50$
   B) $2\sqrt{25}$
   C) $2\sqrt{5}$
   D) $5\sqrt{2}$

Step 1: Factor the number inside the square root sign. Step 2: Look to see if any of the factors are perfect squares. In this case, the only factor that is a perfect square is 25. Step 3: Find the square root of 25 then simplify.

25) $\sqrt{36} + 4\sqrt{72} - 2\sqrt{144} = ?$
   A) $2\sqrt{36}$
   B) $2\sqrt{252}$
   C) $18 + 24\sqrt{2}$
   D) $-18 + 24\sqrt{2}$

Step 1: Find the common factors that are perfect squares. Step 2: Factor the amounts inside each of the radical signs and simplify.

26) $\sqrt{7} \times \sqrt{11} = ?$
   A) $\sqrt{77}$
   B) $\sqrt{18}$
   C) $7\sqrt{11}$
   D) $11\sqrt{7}$

Step 1: Multiply the numbers inside the radical signs. Step 2: Put this product inside a radical symbol for your answer.

27) Express as a rational number: $\sqrt[3]{\dfrac{216}{27}}$

   A) 3
   B) 2
   C) $\dfrac{7}{3}$
   D) $\sqrt[3]{2}$

Step 1: Find the cube roots of the numerator and denominator to eliminate the radical. Step 2: Simplify further if possible. The cube root is a number that equals the required product when multiplied by itself two times.

Exponent Laws

28) $7^5 \times 7^3 = ?$

       A) 7^8

       B) 7^{15}

       C) 14^8

       D) 49^8

If the base number is the same, you need to add the exponents when multiplying, but keep the base number the same as before.

29) $xy^6 \div xy^3 = ?$

       A) xy^{18}

       B) xy^3

       C) $x^2 y^3$

       D) xy^2

If the base number is the same, you need to subtract the exponents when dividing, but keep the base number the same as before.

30)   A rocket flies at a speed of 1.7×10^5 miles per hour for 2×10^{-1} hours. How far has this rocket gone?

       A) 340,000 miles

       B) 34,000 miles

       C) 3,400 miles

       D) 340 miles

Step 1: Add the exponents to multiply the 10's. Step 2: Multiply the miles per hour by the number of hours to get the distance traveled. Step 3: Then multiply these two results together to solve the problem.

31) $\sqrt{x^{\frac{5}{7}}} = ?$

       A) $\dfrac{5x}{7}$

       B) $\left(\sqrt[5]{x}\right)^7$

       C) $\left(7\sqrt{x}\right)^5$

       D) $\left(\sqrt[7]{x}\right)^5$

Step 1: Put the base number inside the radical sign. Step 2: The denominator of the exponent is the nth root of the radical. Step 3: The numerator is the new exponent.

32) $x^{-5} = ?$

 A) $\dfrac{1}{x^{-5}}$

 B) $\dfrac{1}{x^5}$

 C) $-5x$

 D) $\dfrac{1}{5x}$

Step 1: Set up a fraction, where 1 is the numerator. Step 2: Put the term with the exponent in the denominator, but remove the negative sign on the exponent.

33) $62^0 = ?$
 A) -62
 B) 0
 C) 1
 D) 62

Any non-zero number raised to the power of zero is equal to 1.

Simplifying Rational Algebraic Expressions

34) $\dfrac{b + \frac{2}{7}}{\frac{1}{b}} = ?$

 A) $b^2 + \dfrac{7}{2}$

 B) $2b + \dfrac{7}{2}$

 C) $b^2 + \dfrac{2b}{7}$

 D) $\dfrac{b}{b + \frac{2}{7}}$

Step 1: When the expression has fractions in both the numerator and denominator, treat the line in the main fraction as the division symbol. Step 2: Invert the fraction that was in the denominator and multiply.

35) $\dfrac{x^2}{x^2 + 2x} + \dfrac{8}{x} = ?$

 A) $\dfrac{x + 8x + 16}{x^2 + 2x}$

 B) $\dfrac{x^2 + 8}{x^2 + 3x}$

 C) $\dfrac{8x^2 + 16x}{x^3}$

 D) $\dfrac{x^2 + 8x + 16}{x^2 + 2x}$

Step 1: Find the lowest common denominator. Since x is common to both denominators, we can convert the denominator of the second fraction to the LCD by multiplying the numerator and denominator of the second fraction by (x + 2). Step 2: When you have both fractions in the LCD, add the numerators to solve.

Factoring Polynomials

36) Perform the operation and simplify: $\dfrac{2a^3}{7} \times \dfrac{3}{a^2} = ?$

   A) $\dfrac{6a}{7}$

   B) $\dfrac{5a^3}{7a^2}$

   C) $\dfrac{2a^6}{21}$

   D) $\dfrac{21}{2a^6}$

Step 1: Multiply the numerator of the first fraction by the numerator of the second fraction to get the new numerator. Step 2: Then multiply the denominators. Step 3: Factor out a^2. Step 4: Simplify.

37) $\dfrac{8x + 8}{x^4} \div \dfrac{5x + 5}{x^2} = ?$

   A) $\dfrac{5x^2}{8}$

   B) $\dfrac{8}{5x^2}$

   C) $\dfrac{3x+3}{x^2}$

   D) $\dfrac{x^2 + 8x + 8}{x^4 + 5x + 5}$

Step 1: Invert and multiply by the second fraction. Step 2: Cancel out (x + 1). Step 3: Cancel out x^2.

Expanding Polynomials

38) Which of the following expressions is equivalent to $(x + 4y)^2$?
   A) $2(x + 8y)$
   B) $2x + 8y$
   C) $x^2 + 8xy^2 + 16y^2$
   D) $x^2 + 8xy + 16y^2$

When expanding polynomials, you should use the FOIL method: First – Outside – Inside – Last.
We can demonstrate the FOIL method on an example equation as follows:
$(a + b)(c + d) = (a \times c) + (a \times d) + (b \times c) + (b \times d) = ac + ad + bc + bd$

Linear Equations

39) A mother has noticed that the more sugar her child eats, the more her child sleeps at night. Which of the following graphs best illustrates the relationship between the amount of sugar the child consumes and the child's amount of sleep?

A)

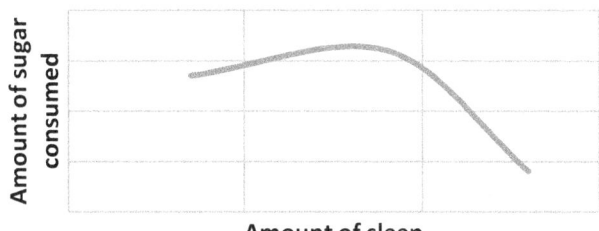

B)

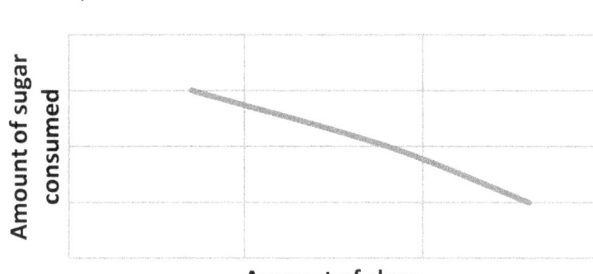

C)

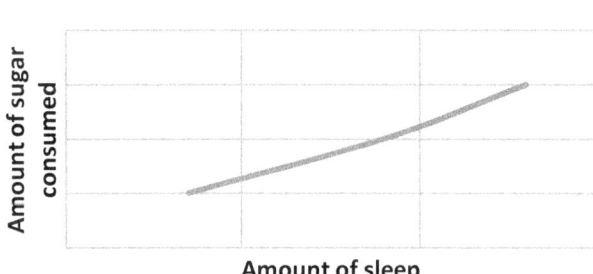

D)

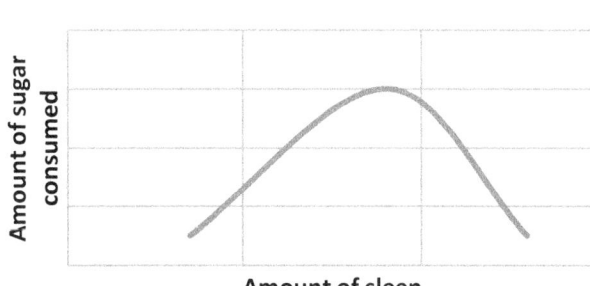

You will need to know the difference between positive linear relationships and negative linear relationships for the exam. In a positive linear relationship, an increase in one variable causes an increase in the other variable, meaning that the line will point upwards from left to right.

In a negative linear relationship, an increase in one variable causes a decrease in the other variable, meaning that the line will point downwards from left to right.

Algebraic Functions

40) The graph of a linear equation is shown below. Which one of the tables of values best represents the points on the graph?

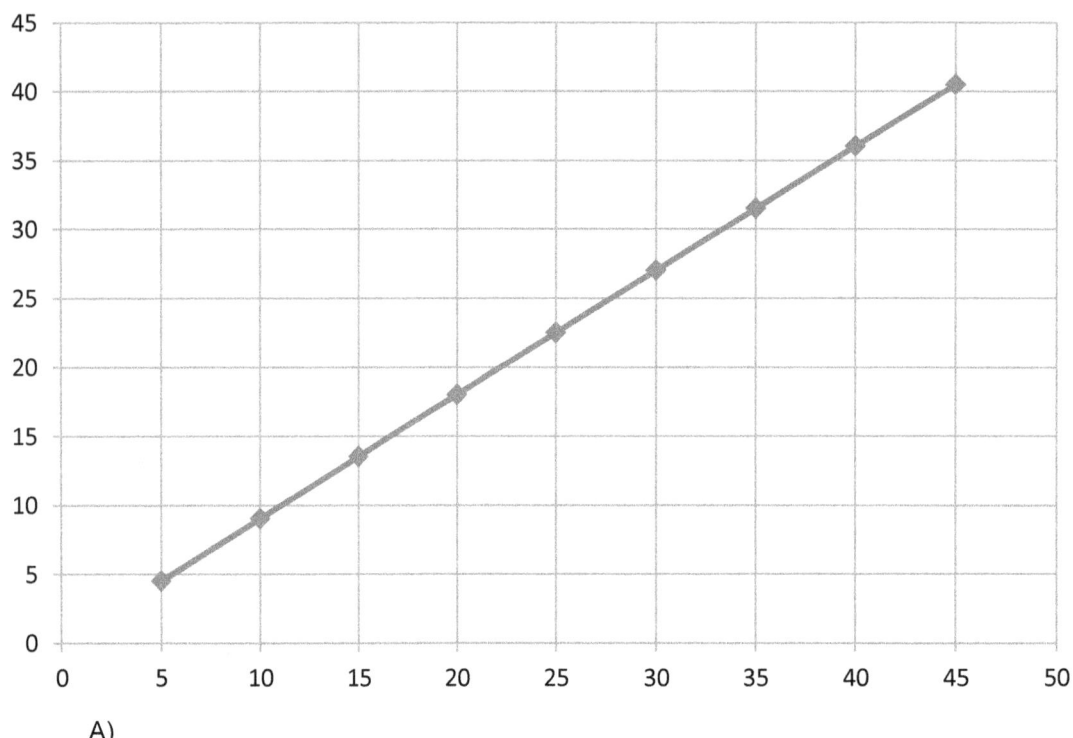

A)

x	y
5	5
10	10
15	15
20	20

B)

x	y
5	4
10	8
15	12
20	16

C)

x	y
5	4.5
10	9
15	13.5
20	18

D)

x	y
5	9
10	13
15	15
20	20

This is an example of an exam question involving algebraic functions. You will have questions on algebraic, polynomial, exponential, and logarithmic functions on your exam. A function expresses the mathematical relationship between x and y. So, a certain recurring mathematical operation on x will yield the output of y. Step 1: Look carefully at the point that is furthest to the left on the graph. You will be able to eliminate several of the answer choices because they will not state this first coordinate correctly.
Step 2: Try to work out the relationship between the coordinates of the first point to those of the next point on the line. Use the horizontal and vertical grid lines on the graph to help you.

Quadratic Equations

41) Simplify: $(x - y)(x + y)$

   A) $x^2 - 2xy - y^2$

   B) $x^2 + 2xy - y^2$

   C) $x^2 + y^2$

   D) $x^2 - y^2$

Use the FOIL method on quadratic equations like this one when the instructions tell you to simplify.

Linear Inequalities

42) $50 - \dfrac{3x}{5} \geq 41$, then $x \leq$?
   A) 15
   B) 25
   C) 41
   D) 50

Step 1: Isolate the whole numbers to one side of the inequality. Step 2: Get rid of the fraction by multiplying each side by 5. Step 3: Divide to simplify further. Step 4: Isolate the variable to solve.

43) The cost of one wizfit is equal to y. If $x - 2 > 5$ and $y = x - 2$, then the cost of 2 wizfits is greater than which one of the following?
   A) $x - 2$
   B) $x - 5$
   C) $y + 5$
   D) 10

Look to see if the inequality and the equation have any variables or terms in common. In this problem, both the inequality and the equation contain $x - 2$. The cost of one wizfit is represented by y, and y is equal to $x - 2$. So, we can substitute values from the equation to the inequality.

Quadratic Inequalities

44) Solve for x: $x^2 - 9 < 0$
   A) $x < -3$ or $x > 3$
   B) $x > -3$ or $x < 3$
   C) $x < -3$ or $x < 3$
   D) $x > -3$ or $x > 3$

For quadratic inequality problems like this one, you need to factor the inequality first. We know that the factors of –9 are: –1 × 9; –3 × 3; 1 × –9. We do not have a term with only the x variable, so we need factors that add up to zero. –3 + 3 = 0. So, try to solve the problem based on these facts. Be sure to check your work when you have found a solution.

Systems of Equations

45) What ordered pair is a solution to the following system of equations?
   $x + y = 7$
   $xy = 12$
   A) (2, 6)
   B) (6, 2)
   C) (4, 2)
   D) (3, 4)

Step 1: Look at the multiplication equation and find the factors of 12. Step 2: Add the factors in each set together to see if they equal 7 to solve the addition in the first equation.

46) Solve by elimination: $3x + 3y = 15$ and $x + 2y = 8$
   A) $x = -18$ and $y = 13$
   B) $x = -2$ and $y = 3$
   C) $x = 2$ and $y = 3$
   D) $x = 3$ and $y = 2$

Step 1: Look at the x term of the first equation, which is 3x. In order to eliminate the x variable, we need to multiply the second equation by 3. Step 2: Subtract this result from the first equation to solve.

Coordinate Geometry

47) If store A is represented by the coordinates (−4, 2) and store B is represented by the coordinates (8,−6), and store A and store B are connected by a line segment, what is the midpoint of this line?
   A) (2, 2)
   B) (2, −2)
   C) (−2, 2)
   D) (−2, −2)

The midpoint of two points on a two-dimensional graph is calculated by using the midpoint formula: $(x_1 + x_2) \div 2$, $(y_1 + y_2) \div 2$

48) What is the distance between (2, 3) and (6, 7)?
   A) 4
   B) 16
   C) $\sqrt{16}$
   D) $\sqrt{32}$

The distance formula is used to calculate the linear distance between two points on a two-dimensional graph. The two points are represented by the coordinates (x_1, y_1) and (x_2, y_2).
$d = \sqrt{(x_2 - x_1)^2 + (y_2 - y_1)^2}$

49) The measurements of a mountain can be placed on a two dimensional linear graph on which $x = 5$ and $y = 315$. If the line crosses the y axis at 15, what is the slope of this mountain?
   A) 60
   B) 63
   C) 300
   D) 315

The slope formula: $m = \dfrac{y_2 - y_1}{x_2 - x_1}$

The slope-intercept formula: $y = mx + b$, where m is the slope and b is the y intercept.

50) Find the x and y intercepts of the following equation: $x^2 + 2y^2 = 144$

A) (12, 0) and (0, $\sqrt{72}$)

B) (0, 12) and ($\sqrt{72}$, 0)

C) (0, $\sqrt{72}$) and (0, 12)

D) (12, 0) and ($\sqrt{72}$, 0)

For questions about x and y intercepts, substitute 0 for y in the equation provided. Then substitute 0 for x to solve the problem.

PERT Math Practice Test Set 2 – Questions 51 to 100:

51) A class which has *x* students. *s*% of the students have been absent this semester. Which of the following equations represents the number of students who have not been absent this semester?
    A) $100(s - x)$
    B) $(100\% - s\%) \times x$
    C) $(100\% - s\%) \div x$
    D) $(1 - s)x$

52) What is 1,594 + 23,786?
    A) 24,380
    B) 25,380
    C) 24.270
    D) 25,270

53) If the value of x is between 0.0007 and 0.0021, which of the following could be x?
    A) 0.0012
    B) 0.0006
    C) 0.0022
    D) 0.022

54) The total funds, represented by variable F, available for P charity projects is represented by the equation F = $500P + $3,700. If the charity has $40,000 available for projects, what is the greatest number of projects that can be completed?
    A) 72
    B) 73
    C) 74
    D) 79

55) Which of the following shows the numbers ordered from greatest to least?
    A) $-1/3, 1/7, 1, 1/5$
    B) $-1/3, 1/7, 1/5, 1$
    C) $-1/3, 1, 1/7, 1/5$
    D) $1, 1/5, 1/7, -1/3$

56) During each flight, a flight attendant must count the number of passengers on board the aircraft. The morning flight had 52 passengers more than the evening flight, and there were 540 passengers in total on the two flights that day. How many passengers were there on the evening flight?
    A) 244
    B) 296
    C) 488
    D) 540

57) A cafeteria serves spaghetti to senior citizens on Fridays. The spaghetti comes prepared in large containers, and each container holds 15 servings of spaghetti. The cafeteria is expecting 82 senior citizens this Friday. What is the least number of containers of spaghetti that the cafeteria will need in order to serve all 82 people?
A) 4
B) 5
C) 6
D) 7

58) A caterpillar travels 10.5 inches in 45 seconds. How far will it travel in 6 minutes?
A) 45 inches
B) 63 inches
C) 64 inches
D) 84 inches

59) Which one of the values will correctly satisfy the following mathematical statement:
$2/3 < ? < 7/9$
A) $1/3$
B) $1/5$
C) $2/6$
D) $7/10$

60) If $\frac{x}{24}$ is between 8 and 9, which of the following could be the value of x?
A) 190
B) 191
C) 200
D) 217

61) At the beginning of class, $1/5$ of the students leave to go to singing lessons. Then $1/4$ of the remaining students leave to go to the principal's office. If 18 students are then left in the class, how many students were there at the beginning of class?
A) 90
B) 45
C) 30
D) 25

62) A dance academy had 300 students at the beginning of January. It lost 5% of its students during the month. However, 15 new students joined the academy on the last day of the month. If this pattern continues for the next two months, how many students will there be at the academy at the end of March?
A) 285
B) 300
C) 310
D) 315

63) The price of a wool coat is reduced 12.5% at the end of the winter. If the original price of the coat was $120, what will the price be after the reduction?
   A) $108.00
   B) $107.50
   C) $105.70
   D) $105.00

64) A motorcycle traveled 38.4 miles in $4/5$ of an hour. What was the approximate speed of the motorcycle in miles per hour?
   A) 9.6
   B) 30.72
   C) 48
   D) 52

65) A factory that makes microchips produces 20 times as many functioning chips as defective chips. If the factory produced 11,235 chips in total last week, how many of them were defective?
   A) 535
   B) 561
   C) 1,070
   D) 10,700

66) A company mixes chemicals in a tank to make a sealing treatment for driveways. The company measures each additive in decimal units, with 100 units representing the filled tank. The tank contains 75.25 units of Chemical X, 10.75 units of Chemical Y, and 3.20 units of Chemical Z. Which of the following represents, in terms of units, how full the tank currently is?
   A) 99.2
   B) 89.2
   C) 88.3
   D) 80.2

67) A company's online survey results show that 45% of its online reviews are 5-star and 35% of its online reviews are 4-star. What percentage below represents the total amount of online 5-star and 4-star reviews?
   A) 80%
   B) 70%
   C) 45%
   D) 35%

68) A home decorating business has just received an order for 5 holders for tea-light candles. Each tea-light candle holder takes $2^1/_2$ hours to make. How much time is needed to make all five holders?
   A) 10 hours and 25 minutes
   B) 10 hours and 30 minutes
   C) 10 hours and 50 minutes
   D) 12 hours and 30 minutes

69) A stationery store sells high quality pens and pencils. After taking inventory this morning, the manager has determined that there are 350 pens in stock. 500 pens should be in stock. The store started the month with 105 pens in stock. 400 pens were purchased after the start of the month. You want to determine how many pens have sold so far this month. Which item below best represents the starting point for solving this problem?
A) number of pens sold last month
B) number of pens in stock
C) number of pens at the beginning of the month
D) number of pens needed to replenish stock

70) A road maintenance contractor has a contract to paint lines on the highways and county roads for the county. It needs to paint lines on 500 miles of roads once every 6 years. It needs to paint a double white line down the center of all 500 miles of the roads. On 200 miles of these roads, it also need to paint a single yellow line on the left-side of the road. How many miles of yellow and white lines will the company need to paint over the next 12 years?
A) 700
B) 900
C) 1400
D) 2400

71) A town has recently suffered a flood. The total cost, represented by variable C, which is available to accommodate R number of residents in emergency housing is represented by the equation C = \$750R + \$2,550. If the town has a total of \$55,000 available for emergency housing, what is the greatest number of residents that it can house?
A) 68
B) 69
C) 70
D) 71

72) Solve for x: $x^2 - 5x + 6 \leq 0$
A) $2 \geq x \geq 3$
B) $2 \leq x \leq 3$
C) $x < -3$ or $x < 2$
D) $x > -2$ or $x > 3$

73) $x^2 + xy - y = 254$ and $x = 12$. What is the value of y?
A) 110
B) 10
C) 11
D) 12

74) $(3x + y)(x - 5y) = ?$
A) $3x^2 - 14xy - 5y^2$
B) $3x^2 - 14xy + 5y^2$
C) $3x^2 + 14xy - 5y^2$
D) $3x^2 + 14xy + 5y^2$

75) Factor: $9x^3 - 3x$
    A) $3x(3x^2 - 1)$
    B) $3x(3x - 1)$
    C) $3x(x^2 - 1)$
    D) $3x(x - 3)$

76) Which of the following statements is true with respect to the lined graph below?

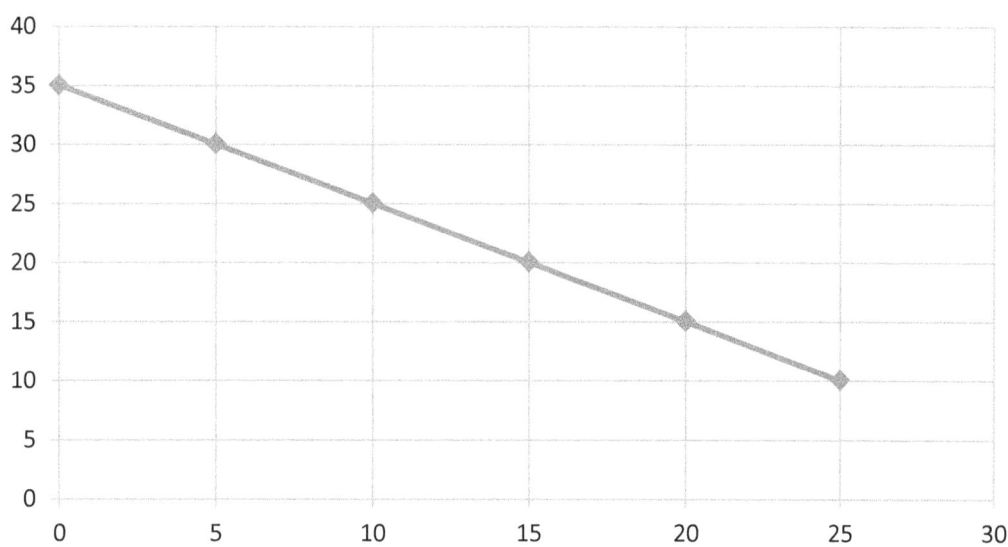

   A) The line has a slope of −1 and contains point (20, 15).
   B) The line has a slope of 1 and contains point (20, 15).
   C) The line has a slope of −1 and contains point (15, 20).
   D) The line has a slope of 1 and contains point (15, 20).

77) Simplify: $\sqrt{15} + 3\sqrt{15}$
    A) 45
    B) $4\sqrt{15}$
    C) $2\sqrt{15}$
    D) $3\sqrt{30}$

78) $\sqrt{5} \times \sqrt{3}$ = ?
    A) 15
    B) $\sqrt{8}$
    C) $\sqrt{15}$
    D) $5\sqrt{3}$

79) Which of the following expressions is equivalent to $\frac{x}{5} + \frac{y}{2}$?

    A) $\frac{x+y}{7}$

    B) $\frac{2x+5y}{10}$

C) $\frac{5x + 2y}{10}$

D) $\frac{2x + 5y}{7}$

80) What equation represents the slope-intercept formula for the following data?

Through (4, 5); $m = -\frac{3}{5}$

A) $y = -\frac{3}{5}x + 5$

B) $y = -\frac{12}{5}x - 5$

C) $y = -\frac{3}{5}x - \frac{37}{5}$

D) $y = -\frac{3}{5}x + \frac{37}{5}$

81) Which of the following is equivalent to: $\frac{x^2 + 5x + 4}{x^2 + 6x + 5} \times \frac{16}{x + 5}$?

A) $\frac{16x + 64}{x + 5}$

B) $\frac{x + 20}{x + 5}$

C) $\frac{x + 20}{x^2 + 10x + 25}$

D) $\frac{16x + 64}{x^2 + 10x + 25}$

82) Which of the following is equivalent to: $\frac{8x - 8}{x} \div \frac{3x - 3}{6x^2}$?

A) $\frac{3x^2 - 3x}{48x^3 - 48x^2}$

B) $\frac{5x - 5}{6x^2}$

C) $\frac{8(x-1) \times 6x^2}{x \times 3(x-1)}$

D) $16x$

83) $(25x)^0 = ?$
A) 0
B) 5
C) 1
D) 25

84) $4^{11} \times 4^8 = ?$

   A) 16^{19}

   B) 4^{19}

   C) 8^{19}

   D) 4^{88}

85) $\sqrt{8x^4} \cdot \sqrt{32x^6} = ?$

   A) $8\sqrt{32x^{10}}$

   B) $16x^{10}$

   C) $16x^5$

   D) $256x^{10}$

86) State the x and y intercepts that fall on the straight line represented by the equation: $y = x + 14$
   A) (−14, 0) and (0, 14)
   B) (0, 14) and (0, −14)
   C) (14, 0) and (0, −14)
   D) (0, −14) and (14, 0)

87) Find the midpoint of the line segment that connects the points (5, 2) and (7, 4).
   A) (6, 3)
   B) (3, 6)
   C) (3.5, 5.5)
   D) (12, 6)

88) A plumber charges $100 per job, plus $25 per hour worked. He is going to do 5 jobs this month. He will earn a total of $4,000. How many hours will he work this month?
   A) 32
   B) 40
   C) 140
   D) 160

89) $\left(2 + \sqrt{6}\right)^2 = ?$
   A) 8
   B) $8 + 2\sqrt{6}$
   C) $8 + 4\sqrt{6}$
   D) $10 + 4\sqrt{6}$

90) In the xy plane, a line crosses the y axis at point (0, 4) and passes through point (6, 8). Which one of the following could be an equation of the line?

A) $y = \frac{3}{2}x + 4$

B) $y = \frac{2}{3}x + 0$

C) $y = \frac{3}{2}x + 0$

D) $y = \frac{2}{3}x + 4$

91) The figure in the xy plane below is going to be moved 7 units to the right and 6 units down. What will the coordinates of point C be after the shift?

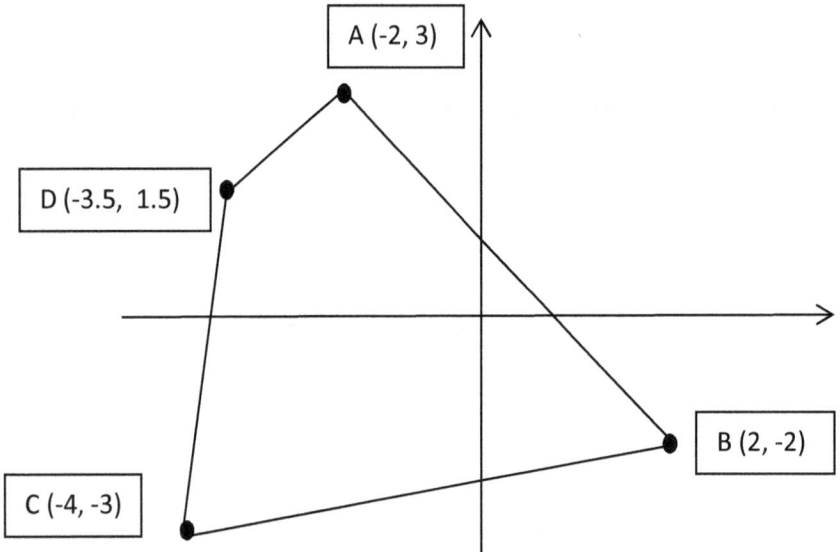

A) (3, 3) B) (9, –8) C) (3, –9) D) (–11, –9)

92) Mustafa bought 4 quarts of cranberry juice for $3 per quart and x quarts of orange juice for $2 per quart. The average cost of both drinks can be represented by the equation ($12 + $2x) ÷ (4 + x). If the equation ($12 + $2x) ÷ (4 + x) is graphed in the xy plane, what quantity will be plotted at the y intercept of the graph?

A) 5

B) 4

C) 3

D) 2

93) Toby is going to buy a car. The total purchase price of the car, including interest, is represented by variable C. He will pay D dollars immediately, and then he will make equal payments (P) each month for a certain number of months (M). Which equation below represents the amount of his monthly payment (P)?

A) $\frac{C-D}{M}$

B) $\frac{C}{M} - D$

C) $\frac{M}{C-D}$

D) $D - \frac{C}{M}$

94) There are three boys in a family, named Alex, Burt, and Zander. Alex is twice as old as Burt, and Burt is one year older than three times the age of Zander. Which of the following statements best describes the relationship between the ages of the boys?
A) Alex is 4 years older than 6 times the age of Zander.
B) Alex is 2 years older than 6 times the age of Zander.
C) Alex is 4 years older than 3 times the age of Zander.
D) Alex is 2 years older than 3 times the age of Zander.

95) The price of a sofa at a local furniture store was x dollars on Wednesday this week. On Thursday, the price of the sofa was reduced by 10% of Wednesday's price. On Friday, the price of the sofa was reduced again by 15% of Thursday's price. Which of the following expressions can be used to calculate the price of the sofa on Friday?
A) $(0.75)x$
B) $(0.10)(0.15)x$
C) $(0.10)(0.85)x$
D) $(0.90)(0.85)x$

96) A toy store can buy 350 units of a particular type of toy from one supplier for 85 cents each or from a different supplier for $295 for all 350 units. The store will have to pay a sales tax of 8.5% on either purchase. If the store chooses the best price for the toys, including tax, how much will it pay in total?
A) $295.00
B) $297.50
C) $320.08
D) $320.29

97) A business has received $123 off an order. This amounted to a 40% discount off the original price. How much would the business have paid without the discount?
A) $30.75
B) $49.20
C) $205.00
D) $307.50

98) A company that supplies food products to caterers buys tomato sauce by the crate. A crate containing 100 cans of tomato sauce weighs 90 pounds and 12 ounces. The crate weighs 15 pounds when it is empty. Each can of tomato sauce weighs 12 ounces. Approximately how many cans of tomato sauce are in the crate?
A) 101
B) 121
C) 139
D) 1200

99) A company in your local area sells different types of rope. The rope comes in coiled bundles that are labeled with the number of feet in each bundle. The company needs to change the labels so that they show the length of each one in millimeters. What formula should be used? (1 foot = 0.3048 meters)
A) millimeters = feet × 0.3048
B) millimeters = feet × 0.3048 × 1,000
C) millimeters = feet ÷ 0.3048
D) millimeters = feet × 0.3048 ÷ 1,000

100) A land surveyor measures farmland for the county deeds office. The surveying equipment she uses reports the result in terms of square yards. However, she needs to convert the measurements to acres for the report you have to prepare. Which formula should she use?
(1 acre = 43,560 square feet)
A) acres = (square yards × 9) ÷ 43,560
B) acres = (square yards × 9) × 43,560
C) acres = (square yards ÷ 9) ÷ 43,560
D) acres = (square yards ÷ 9) × 43,560

PERT Math Practice Test Set 3 – Questions 101 to 150

101) The numbers in the following list are ordered from least to greatest: α, $2/7$, $8/9$, 1.35, $11/3$, μ
    Which of the following could be the value of μ?
    A) 3.5
    B) $10/4$
    C) 4.1
    D) $1/6$

102) $82 + 9 \div 3 - 5 = ?$
    A) −40.50
    B) 40.50
    C) 80.00
    D) 85.33

103) $52 + 6 \times 3 - 48 = ?$
    A) 22
    B) 82
    C) 126
    D) 322

104) Convert the following to a decimal: $4/16$
    A) 0.0025
    B) 0.025
    C) 0.25
    D) 0.40

105) 90 is 30 percent of what number?
    A) 27
    B) 120
    C) 0.0375
    D) 300

106) $6\tfrac{3}{4} - 2\tfrac{1}{2} = ?$
    A) $4\tfrac{1}{4}$
    B) $4\tfrac{3}{8}$
    C) $4\tfrac{5}{8}$
    D) $4\tfrac{6}{8}$

107) $9 \times 6 + 42 \div 6 = ?$
    A) 8
    B) 16
    C) 27
    D) 61

108) The local Boy Scouts has 31 members. If each member contributes 12 cans of food for a food drive, how many cans of food are contributed in total?
A) 472
B) 372
C) 132
D) 43

109) $1/8 \div 4/3 = ?$
A) $1/6$
B) $32/3$
C) $3/24$
D) $3/32$

110) A group of friends are trying to lose weight. Person A lost $14^3/_4$ pounds. Person B lost $20^1/_5$ pounds. Person C lost 36.35 pounds. What is the total weight loss for the group?
A) 70.475
B) 71.05
C) 71.15
D) 71.30

111) Convert the following fraction to decimal format: $5/50$
A) 0.0010
B) 0.0100
C) 0.1000
D) 0.0500

112) What is the remainder when 600 is divided by 9?
A) 0.66
B) 0.67
C) 7
D) 6

113) $3^1/_2 - 2^3/_5 = ?$
A) $9/10$
B) $1^1/_{10}$
C) $1^1/_3$
D) $1^2/_3$

114) A climatologist needs to calculate the average high temperature in one city over a five-day period in degrees Celsius. However, the high temperatures are reported in Fahrenheit. You have collected the following data: Day 1: 72° F; Day 2: 68° F; Day 3: 65° F; Day 4: 82° F; Day 5: 81° F. What was the approximate average high temperature in degrees Celsius? Please note that the formula to convert degrees Fahrenheit to Celsius is as follows: °F = 1.8(°C) + 32
A) 71°C
B) 23°C
C) 74°C
D) 32°C

115) A hairdressing salon provides haircuts, styling, and other services to customers. The manicurist has reported that it takes 5 hours to do 4 full manicures and 2.5 hours to do 5 full pedicures. How long should it take the manicurist to do 20 full manicures and 25 full pedicures?
A) 7 hours and 30 minutes
B) 12 hours and 30 minutes
C) 37 hours and 50 minutes
D) 37 hours and 30 minutes

116) A librarian for a local community college has prepared a recent report on a publishing project which shows that shows that 57.75% of the project has been completed in the past 7 work days. If work continues at the same rate, approximately how many work days will be required in total for the entire project?
A) 9
B) 10
C) 12
D) 14

117) A veterinary practice is trying to find the best deal on some veterinary supplies. The practice wants to purchase 135 units of a certain feline medication. One company charges $15.30 per unit, plus 6% sales tax. Another company charges $2,100 for the whole order plus a $75 administration charge, but does not charge sales tax. If the practice chooses the best price, how much will it pay for the medication?
A) $2,065.50
B) $2,100.00
C) $2,175.00
D) $2,189.43

118) $1/6 + (1/2 \div 3/8) - (1/3 \times 3/2) = ?$
A) $23/6$
B) 1
C) 2
D) $1/10$

119) Mary needs to get $650 in donations. So far, she has obtained 80% of the money she needs. How much money does she still need?
A) $8.19
B) $13.00
C) $32.50
D) $130.00

120) The Abdul family is shopping at a superstore. They buy product A and product B. Product A costs $5 each, and product B costs $8 each. They buy 4 of product A. They also buy a certain quantity of product B. The total value of their purchase is $60. How many units of product B did they buy?
A) 4
B) 5
C) 6
D) 8

121) A hockey team had 50 games this season and lost 20 percent of them. How many games did the team win?
   A) 8
   B) 10
   C) 20
   D) 40

122) Jonathan can run 3 miles in 25 minutes. If he maintains this pace, how long will it take him to run 12 miles?
   A) 1 hour and 15 minutes
   B) 1 hour and 40 minutes
   C) 1 hour and 45 minutes
   D) 3 hours

123) Mrs. Johnson is going to give candy to the students in her class. The first bag of candy that she has contains 43 pieces. The second contains 28 pieces, and the third contains 31 pieces. If there are 34 students in Mrs. Johnson's class, and the candy is divided equally among all of the students, how many pieces of candy will each student receive?
   A) 3 pieces
   B) 4 pieces
   C) 5 pieces
   D) 51 pieces

124) Use the table below to answer the following question:

Sunday	Monday	Tuesday	Wednesday	Thursday	Friday	Saturday
−10°F	−9°F	1°F	6°F	8°F	13°F	12°F

The weather forecast for the coming week is given in the table above. What is the difference between the highest and lowest forecasted temperatures for the week?
   A) −2°F
   B) −3°F
   C) 3°F
   D) 23°F

125) Expand the polynomial: $(x - 5)(3x + 8)$
   A) $3x^2 - 7x - 40$
   B) $3x^2 - 7x + 40$
   C) $3x^2 + 23x - 40$
   D) $3x^2 + 23x + 40$

126) If $\frac{3}{4}x - 2 = 4$, $x = ?$

A) $\frac{8}{3}$

B) $\frac{1}{8}$

C) 8

D) −8

127) Solve for x: $x^2 + 2x - 8 \leq 0$
A) $-4 \geq x \geq 2$

B) $-4 \geq x \leq 2$

C) $-4 \leq x \geq 2$

D) $-4 \leq x \leq 2$

128) If $x - 15 > 0$ and $y = x - 15$, then $y > ?$
A) x
B) $x + 15$
C) $x - 15$
D) 0

129) Which of the following is equivalent to the expression $2(x + 2)(x - 3)$ for all values of x?
A) $2x^2 - 2x - 12$
B) $2x^2 - 10x - 6$
C) $2x^2 + 2x - 12$
D) $2x^2 + 10x - 6$

130) Which of the following is a factor of: $2xy - 6x^2y + 4x^2y^2$
A) $(1 + 3x - 2xy)$
B) $(1 - 3x + 2xy)$
C) $(1 + 3x + 2xy)$
D) $(1 - 3x - 2xy)$

131) A construction company is building new homes on a housing development. It has an agreement with the municipality that H number of houses must be built every 30 days. If H number of houses are not built during the 30 day period, the company has to pay a penalty to the municipality of P dollars per house. The penalty is paid per house for the number of houses that fall short of the 30-day target. If A represents the actual number of houses built during the 30-day period, which equation below can be used to calculate the penalty for the 30-day period?
A) $(H - P) \times 30$
B) $(H - A) \times P$
C) $(A - H) \times 30$
D) $(A - H) \times P$

132) Perform the operation: $(5ab - 6a)(3ab^3 - 4b^2 - 3a)$
 A) $15a^2b^4 - 20ab^3 - 15a^2b - 18a^2b^3 - 24ab^2 - 18a^2$
 B) $15a^2b^4 - 20ab^3 - 15a^2b - 18a^2b^3 + 24ab^2 + 18a^2$
 C) $15a^2b^4 - 20ab^3 - 15a^2b - 18a^2b^3 - 24ab^2 + 18a^2$
 D) $15ab^4 - 20ab^3 - 15a^2b - 18a^2b^3 + 24ab^2 + 18a^2$

133) Which of the following is equivalent to $\frac{x}{5} \div \frac{9}{y}$?

 A) $\frac{xy}{45}$

 B) $\frac{9x}{5y}$

 C) $\frac{1}{9} \times \frac{x}{5y}$

 D) $\frac{1}{5} \times \frac{9}{5y}$

134) Which of the following values of x is a possible solution to the inequality?: $-3x + 14 < 5$
 A) −3.1
 B) 2.80
 C) 2.25
 D) 3.15

135) $(x - 2y)(2x^2 - y) = ?$
 A) $2x^3 - 4x^2y + 2y^2 - xy$
 B) $2x^3 + 2y^2 - 5xy$
 C) $2x^3 - 4x^2y + 2y^2 + xy$
 D) $2x^3 + 4x^2y + 2y^2 - xy$

136) What is the value of the expression $2x^2 + 5xy - y^2$ when $x = 4$ and $y = -3$?
 A) −37
 B) −19
 C) 86
 D) 101

137) If $6 + 8(2\sqrt{x} + 4) = 62$, then $\sqrt{x} = ?$
 A) 3.25
 B) 24
 C) $\frac{3}{2}$
 D) $\frac{2}{3}$

138) $\sqrt{18} \times \sqrt{8} = ?$
   A) $18\sqrt{8}$
   B) $\sqrt{26}$
   C) $\sqrt{12}$
   D) 12

139) If $2(3x - 1) = 4(x + 1) - 3$, what is the value of x?
   A) $3/2$
   B) 3
   C) $2/3$
   D) 2

140) The graph of a linear equation is shown below. Which one of the tables of values best represents the points on the graph?

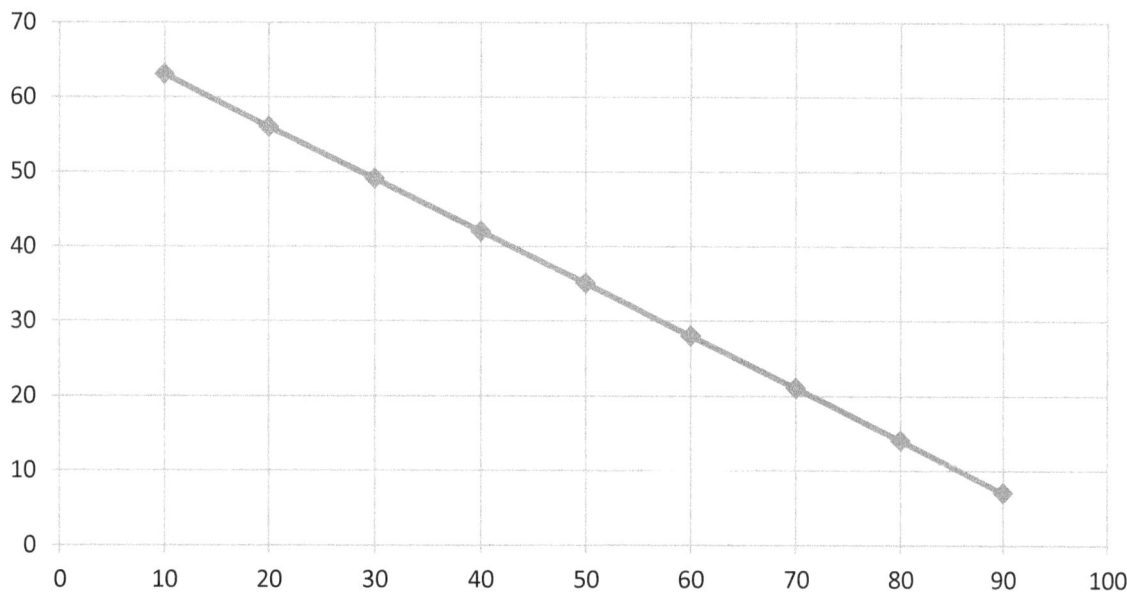

A)

x	y
5	65
10	64
15	63
20	62

B)

x	y
5	68
15	60
25	52
35	54

C)

x	y
10	63
20	56
30	49
40	42

D)

x	y
10	68
20	60
30	52
40	44

141) $20 - \frac{3x}{4} \geq 17$, then $x \leq ?$
 A) −12
 B) −4
 C) −3
 D) 4

142) Which of the following points lies on the graph of $10x + 3y = 29$?
 A) (3, 2)
 B) (2, 3)
 C) (1, 6)
 D) (6, 1)

143) A vegetable grower wants to put to put wooden fence panels around the outside of her vegetable patch. Each panel is 1 yard in length. The patch is rectangular and is 12 yards long and 10 yards wide. How many panels are needed in order to enclose the vegetable patch?
 A) 22
 B) 44
 C) 100
 D) 120

144) Look at the graph below and answer the question that follows.

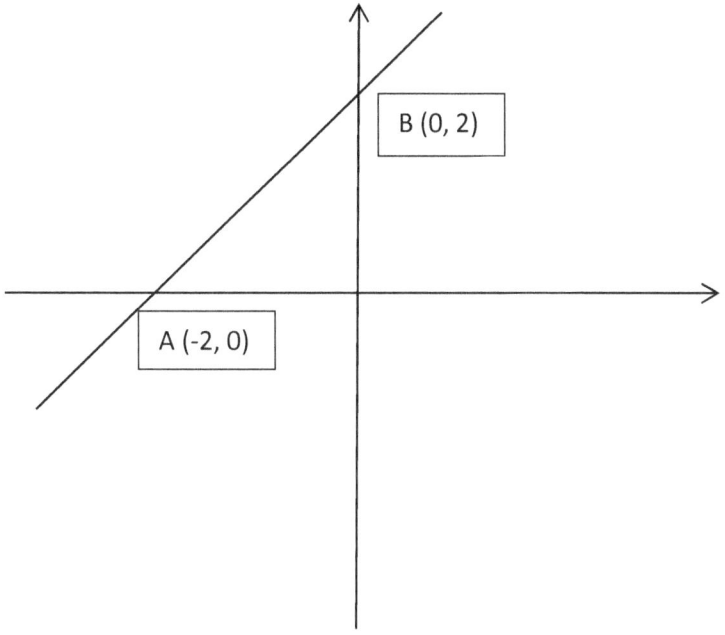

The line in the xy plane above is going to be shifted 5 units to the left and 4 units up. What are the coordinates of point B after the shift?

A) (−5, 6)

B) (5, 6)

C) (5, 4)

D) (−7, 4)

145) In the standard (x, y) plane, what is the distance between $(4\sqrt{7}, -2)$ and $(7\sqrt{7}, 4)$?
A) $3\sqrt{11}$
B) 27
C) 36
D) 99

146) Four members of a family are having a meal in a restaurant. They each have a main dish and a desert. The main dishes are all the same price each, and the deserts are also all the same price for each dessert. The main dishes cost $8 each. The total cost of their meal is $48. How much did each of their deserts cost?
A) $3.75
B) $4
C) $6
D) $22

147) If $f(x) = x^2 + 3x - 8$, what is $f(x+3)$?
   A) $(x+3)^2 + 3x - 8$
   B) $(x+3)^2 + 3(x+3) - 8$
   C) $x^2 + 3x - 5$
   D) $3(x^2 + 3x - 8)$

148) $\sqrt{-16} = ?$
   A) 4
   B) −4
   C) an imaginary number
   D) Cannot be determined

149) A fuel tanker truck has a capacity of 1200 gallons. If it takes 75 minutes to fill the tanker truck, at what rate is it being filled?
   A) 6.25 gallons per minute
   B) 16 gallons per minute
   C) 62.5 gallons per minute
   D) 160 gallons per minute

150) Shawn's final grade for a class is based on his grades from two projects, X and Y. Project X counts toward 45% of his final grade. Project Y counts toward 55% of his final grade. What equation can be used to calculate Shawn's final grade for this class?

   A) .55X + .45Y

   B) .45X + .55Y

   C) (.45X + .55Y) ÷ 2

   D) X + Y

PERT Math Practice Test Set 4 – Questions 151 to 200

151) The number of visitors a museum had on Tuesday (T) was twice as much as the number of visitors it had on Monday (M). The number of visitors it had on Wednesday (W) was 20% greater than that on Tuesday. Which equation can be used to calculate the total number of visitors for the three days?
A) M + 2T + W
B) M + 1.2T + W
C) W + .20W + 2T + M
D) 5.4M

152) Yesterday a train traveled $117\tfrac{3}{4}$ miles. Today it traveled $102\tfrac{1}{6}$ miles. What is the difference between the distance traveled today and yesterday?
A) 15 miles
B) $15\tfrac{1}{4}$ miles
C) $15\tfrac{7}{12}$ miles
D) $15\tfrac{9}{12}$ miles

153) Sam is driving a truck at 70 miles per hour. At 10:30 am, he sees this sign:

Brownsville	35 miles
Dunnstun	70 miles
Farnam	140 miles
Georgetown	210 miles

After Sam sees the sign, he continues to drive at the same speed. At 11:00 am, how far will he be from Farnam?
A) He will be in Farnam.
B) He will be 35 miles from Farnam.
C) He will be 70 miles from Farnam.
D) He will be 105 miles from Farnam.

154) In a math class, $\tfrac{1}{3}$ of the students fail a test. If twelve students have failed the test, how many students are in the class in total?
A) 15
B) 16
C) 36
D) 38

155) Mark owns a bargain bookstore that sells every book for $5. Last week, his sales were $525. This week his sales figure was $600. How many more books did Mark sell this week, compared to last week?
A) 5
B) 15
C) 25
D) 75

156) Kieko needs to calculate 16% of 825. Which of the following formulas can she use?
A) 825 × 16
B) 160 × 825
C) 825 × 1600
D) 825 × 0.16

157) Wei Lei bought a shirt on sale. The original price of the shirt was $18, and he got a 40% discount. What was the sales price of the shirt?
A) $7.20
B) $10.80
C) $11.80
D) $17.60

158) Professor Smith uses a system of extra-credit points for his class. Extra-credit points can be offset against the points lost on an exam due to incorrect responses. David answered 18 questions incorrectly on the exam and lost 36 points. He then earned 25 extra credit points. By how much was his exam score ultimately lowered?
A) −11
B) 11
C) 18
D) 25

159) A blacksmith makes iron railings for homes and exteriors. The railings are made in 1/16 inch increments in diameter. The blacksmith has just made a railing that is 5/8 inch diameter, but he has realized that it is too large for the current project. What size diameter should he try next?
A) 9/16
B) 11/16
C) 13/16
D) 3/4

160) A chain of stores that sell appliances can purchase 120 washing machines from its usual supplier for $172 each. The store can get the same 120 washing machines from a second supplier for $20,500 in total or from a third supplier for $19,000 plus 7% sales tax. How much will the store pay to get the best deal?
A) $19,000
B) $20,330
C) $20,500
D) $20,640

161) The price of an item is normally $22.50, but customers with a membership can purchase it at the discounted price of $20. What percentage best represents the membership discount?
A) 0.125%
B) 12.5%
C) 0.111%
D) 11%

162) The county is proposing a 7.5% increase in its annual real estate tax. If the tax is currently $480 per year, how much would the tax be if the proposed increase is approved?
A) $444
B) $487
C) $516
D) $840

163) Mrs. Ramirez is inviting 12 children to her son's birthday party. The children will play pin the tail on the donkey. Mrs. Ramirez has already made 40 tails for the game. She wants to give each child 4 tails to play the game. How many more tails does she need to make?
A) 4
B) 8
C) 10
D) 12

164) A class contains 20 students. On Tuesday 5% of the students were absent. On Wednesday 20% of the students were absent. How many more students were absent on Wednesday than on Tuesday?
A) 1
B) 2
C) 3
D) 4

165) Records indicate that there were 12 hospitals in Johnson County in 1998, but this number had increased to 15 hospitals in 2016. There were 12 births per hospital in Johnson County in 1998. The total number of births in Johnson County was 240 in 2016. By what amount does the average number of births per hospital in Johnson County for 2016 exceed those for 1998?
A) 3 births per hospital
B) 4 births per hospital
C) 15 births per hospital
D) 16 births per hospital

166) Marta can walk one mile in 17 minutes. At this rate, how long would it take her to walk 5 miles?
A) 1 hour and 5 minutes
B) 1 hour and 7 minutes
C) 1 hour and 8 minutes
D) 1 hour and 25 minutes

167) Sam's final grade for a class is based on his scores from a midterm test (M), a project (P), and a final exam (F). The midterm test counts twice as much as the project, and the final exam counts twice as much as the midterm. Which mathematical expression below can be used to calculate Sam's final grade?
A) P + M + F
B) P + M + 2F
C) P + 2M + F
D) P + 2M + 4F

168) Bart is riding his bike at a rate of 12 miles per hour. He arrives in the town of Wilmington at 3:00 pm. The town of Mount Pleasant is 50 miles from Wilmington. How far will Bart be from Mount Pleasant at 5:00 pm if he continues riding his bike at this speed?
   A) 12 miles
   B) 20 miles
   C) 24 miles
   D) 26 miles

169) A ticket office sold 360 more tickets on Friday than it did on Saturday. If the office sold 2570 tickets in total during Friday and Saturday, how many tickets did it sell on Friday?
   A) 360
   B) 1105
   C) 1465
   D) 1565

170) Tom's height increased by 10% this year. If Tom was 5 feet tall at the beginning of the year, how tall is he now?
   A) 5 feet 1 inch
   B) 5 feet 5 inches
   C) 5 feet 6 inches
   D) 5 feet 10 inches

171) Carlos buys 2 pairs of jeans for $22.98 each. He later decides to exchange both pairs of jeans for 3 sweaters which cost $15.50 each. Which equation can Carlos use to calculate the extra money he will have to pay for the exchange?
   A) 2 × (22.98 - 15.50)
   B) 3 × (22.98 - 15.50)
   C) (3 × 22.98) − (2 × 15.50)
   D) (3 × 15.50) − (2 × 22.98)

172) Jason does the high jump for his high school track and field team. His first jump is at 3.246 meters. His second is 3.331 meters, and his third is 3.328 meters. If the height of each jump is rounded up or down to the nearest one-hundredth of a meter (also called a centimeter), what is the estimate of the total height for all three jumps combined?
   A) 9.80
   B) 9.89
   C) 9.90
   D) 9.91

173) Use the table below to answer the question that follows.

Regional Railway Train Service	
Departure Time	Arrival Time
9:50 am	10:36 am
11:15 am	12:01 pm
12:30 pm	1:16 pm
2:15 pm	3:01 pm
?	5:51 pm

The journey on the Regional Railway is always exactly the same duration. What is the missing time in the chart above?
A) 3:30 pm
B) 4:15 pm
C) 4:30 pm
D) 5:05 pm

174) Captain Smith needs to purchase rope for his fleet of yachts. He owns 26 yachts and needs 6 feet 10 inches of rope for each one. How much rope does he need in total?
A) 152 feet
B) 177 feet 8 inches
C) 257 feet 8 inches
D) 260 feet

175) Find the value of x that solves the following proportion: $3/6 = x/14$
A) 3
B) 6
C) 7
D) 8

176) In a shipment of 100 mp3 players, 1% are faulty. What is the ratio of non-faulty mp3 players to faulty mp3 players?
A) 1:100
B) 100:1
C) 99:100
D) 99:1

177) Solve for x: $x^2 + 4x + 3 > 0$
A) $x < -3$ or $x > -1$
B) $x < -3$ or $x < -1$
C) $x > -3$ or $x < -1$
D) $x > -3$ or $x > -1$

178) The graph below shows the relationship between the number of days of rain per month and the amount of people who exercise outdoors per month. What relationship can be observed?

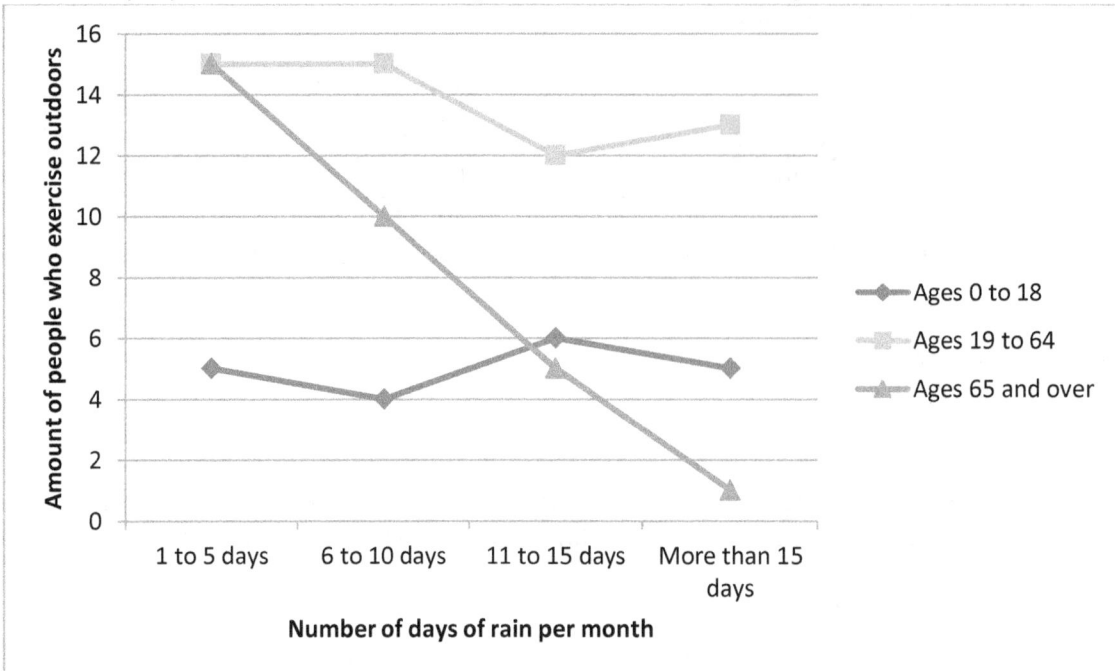

A) Young children are reliant upon an adult in order to exercise outdoors.
B) The exercise habits of working age people seem to fluctuate proportionately to the amount of rainfall.
C) In the 19 to 64 age group, there is a negative relationship between the number of days of rain and the amount of people who exercise outdoors.
D) People aged 65 and over seem less inclined to exercise outdoors when there is more rain.

179) $(x - 9y)^2 = ?$

A) $x^2 + 81y^2$
B) $x^2 - 18xy - 18y^2$
C) $x^2 - 18xy + 81y^2$
D) $x^2 + 18xy - 81y^2$

180) $6 + \frac{x}{4} \geq 22$, then $x \geq ?$

A) −8
B) 64
C) −64
D) 128

181) $(x^2 - x - 12) \div (x - 4) = ?$

A) $(x + 3)$
B) $(x - 3)$
C) $(-x + 3)$
D) $(-x - 3)$

182) Which of the following expressions is equivalent to: $18xy - 24x^2y - 48y^2x^2$?

   A) $6xy(3 - 4x - 8xy)$
   B) $3xy(6 - 8x - 16xy)$
   C) $6x^2y(3 - 4 - 8y)$
   D) $6xy(3 - 4x + 8xy)$

183) $\sqrt{15x^3} \times \sqrt{8x^2}$

   A) $\sqrt{23x^5}$
   B) $2x^2\sqrt{30x^3}$
   C) $2x^2\sqrt{30x}$
   D) $\sqrt{23x^6}$

184) Which one of the following is a solution to the following ordered pairs of equations?
   $-3x - 1 = y$
   $x + 7 = y$
   A) $(5, -2)$
   B) $(-2, 5)$
   C) $(2, 5)$
   D) $(5, 2)$

185) $x^{-4} = ?$
   A) $4\sqrt{x}$
   B) $\sqrt[-4]{x}$
   C) $x^4 \div 1$
   D) $1 \div x^4$

186) If $5(4\sqrt{x} - 8) = 40$, then $x = ?$

   A) $\dfrac{5}{12}$

   B) 4

   C) 16

   D) $\sqrt{\dfrac{5}{12}}$

187) The graph of a line is shown on the xy plane below. The point that has the x-coordinate of 160 is not shown. What is the corresponding y-coordinate of that point?

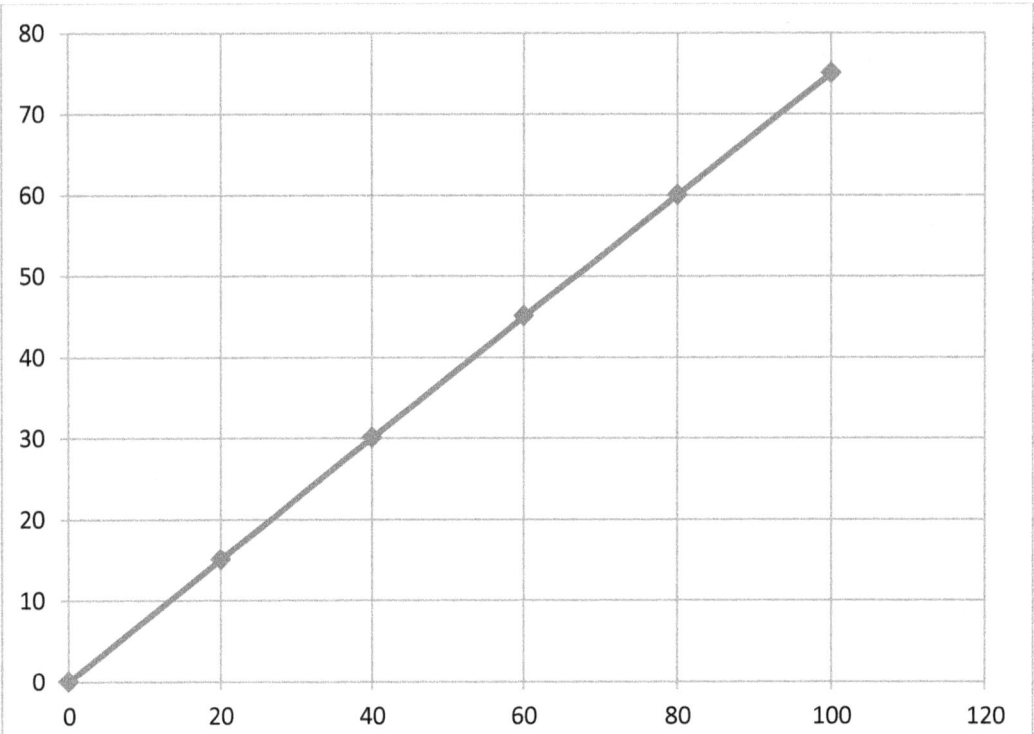

A) 115
B) 120
C) 125
D) 130

188) $-|5-8| = ?$
A) -13
B) 13
C) -3
D) 3

189) Find the x and y intercepts of the following equation: $5x^2 + 4y^2 = 120$

A) $(0, \sqrt{30})$ and $(\sqrt{24}, 0)$

B) $(0, 30)$ and $(24, 0)$

C) $(\sqrt{24}, 0)$ and $(0, \sqrt{30})$

D) $(30, 0)$ and $(0, 24)$

190) Consider a two-dimensional linear graph where x = 4 and y = 15. The line crosses the y axis at 3. What is the slope of this line?

A) $\frac{1}{15}$

B) 3

C) $-\frac{1}{3}$

D) −3

191) Which of the following points lies on the graph of 5x + 6y = 34?
A) (4, 2)
B) (1, 5)
C) (2, 4)
D) (−3, 8)

192) In the xy plane, line L passes through (0, 0) is perpendicular to line K. Line K is represented by the following equation: y = 5x + 0. The equation of line L could be which one of the following?
A) $y = -5x$
B) $y = \frac{1}{5}x + 0$
C) $y = 5x + 0$
D) $y = -\frac{1}{5}x$

193) The price of widgets is $2 each and the price of whatsits is $25 each. Zafira bought widgets and whatsits in one transaction, and she paid $85 in total. If she bought 3 whatsits, how many widgets did she buy?
A) 2
B) 3
C) 5
D) 8

194) $\sqrt{3}$ is equivalent to what number in exponential notation?
A) $3^{\frac{1}{4}}$
B) $3^{\frac{1}{2}}$
C) $1^{\sqrt{3}}$
D) 3^0

195) A participant in a 100 mile endurance event ran at a speed of 5 miles per hour for the first 80 miles of the event and x miles per hour for the last 20 miles of the event. What equation represents the participant's average speed for the entire event?
A) 100 ÷ [(80 ÷ 5) + (20 ÷ x)]
B) 100 × [(80 ÷ 5) + (20 ÷ x)]
C) 100 ÷ [(80 × 5) + (20 × x)]
D) 100 × [(80 × 5) + (20 × x)]

196) Davina is using a recipe that requires 2 cups of sugar for every one-third cup of butter. If she uses 12 cups of sugar, how many cups of butter should she use?
   A) 6 cups of butter
   B) 3 cups of butter
   C) 2 cups of butter
   D) $\frac{1}{3}$ cup of butter

197) A driver travels at 60 miles per hour for two and a half hours before her car fails to start at a service station. She has to wait two hours while the car is repaired before she can continue driving. She then drives at 75 miles an hour for the remainder of her journey. She is traveling to Denver, and her journey is 240 miles in total. If she left home at 6:00 am, what time will she arrive in Denver?
   A) 9:30 am
   B) 11:30 am
   C) 11:42 am
   D) 11:50 am

198) A clothing store sells jackets and jeans at a discount during a sales period. T represents the number of jackets sold and N represents the number of jeans sold. The total amount of money the store collected for sales of jeans and jackets during the sales period was $4,000. The amount of money earned from selling jackets was one-third of that earned from selling jeans. The jeans sold for $20 a pair. How many pairs of jeans did the store sell during the sales period?
   A) 15
   B) 20
   C) 150
   D) 200

199) Which of the following steps will solve the equation for x: $18 = 3(x + 5)$
   A) Subtract 5 from each side of the equation, and then divide both sides by 3.
   B) Subtract 18 from each side of the equation, and then divide both sides by 5.
   C) Multiply both x and 5 by 3 on the right side of the equation. Then subtract 15 from each side of the equation.
   D) Divide each side of the equation by 3. Then subtract 5 from both sides of the equation.

200) Milk fills a tank at a diary at a rate of 3.5 gallons per minute. If the tank has a 500 gallon capacity, approximately how long will it take to fill the tank?
   A) 2 hours and 23 minutes
   B) 2 hours and 13 minutes
   C) 1 hour and 43 minutes
   D) 1 hour and 42 minutes

PERT Math Practice Test Set 5 – Questions 201 to 250

201) It takes Martha 4 hours and 10 minutes to knit one woolen cap. At this rate, how long will it take her to knit 12 caps?
   A) 40 hours
   B) 42 hours
   C) 46 hours
   D) 50 hours

202) The Jones family needs to dig a new well. The well will be 525 feet deep, and it will be topped with a windmill which will be 95 feet in height. What is the distance from the deepest point of the well to the top of the windmill?
   A) 95 feet
   B) 430 feet
   C) 525 feet
   D) 620 feet

203) Mrs. Thompson is having a birthday party for her son. She is going to give balloons to the children. She has one bag that contains 13 balloons, another that contains 22 balloons, and a third that contains 25 balloons. If 12 children are going to attend the party including her son, and the total amount of balloons is to be divided equally among all of the children, how many balloons will each child receive?
   A) 3
   B) 4
   C) 5
   D) 6

204) A bookstore is offering a 15% discount on books. Janet's purchase would be $90 at the normal price. How much will she pay after the discount?
   A) $75.50
   B) $76.50
   C) $77.50
   D) $85.50

205) John is measuring plant growth as part of a botany experiment. Last week, his plant grew 7¾ inches, but this week his plant grew 10½ inches. What is the difference in growth in inches between the two weeks?
   A) 2¼ inches
   B) 2½ inches
   C) 2¾ inches
   D) 3¼ inches

206) Patty works 23 hours a week at a part time job for which she receives $7.50 an hour. She then gets a raise, after which she earns $184 per week. She continues to work 23 hours per week. How much did her hourly pay increase?
A) 50 cents an hour
B) 75 cents an hour
C) $1.00 an hour
D) $8.00 an hour

207) Sheng Li is driving at 70 miles per hour. At 10:00 am, he sees this sign:

Washington	**140 miles**
Yorkville	**105 miles**
Zorster	**210 miles**

He continues driving at the same speed. Where will Sheng Li be at 11:00 am?
A) 70 miles from Washington
B) 105 miles from Washington
C) 75 miles from Yorkville
D) 80 miles from Yorkville

208) Mayumi spent the day counting cars for her job as a traffic controller. In the morning she counted 114 more cars than she did in the afternoon. If she counted 300 cars in total that day, how many cars did she count in the morning?
A) 90
B) 93
C) 114
D) 207

209) Tiffany buys five pairs of socks for $2.50 each. The next day, she decides to exchange these five pairs of socks for four different pairs that cost $3 each. She uses this equation to calculate her refund: (5 × $2.50) – (4 × $3). Which equation below could she have used instead?
A) (5 × 4) – (3 × 2.50)
B) $2.50 – 4($3 – $2.50)
C) (5 × 4) + (3 × 2.50)
D) $3 – (4 × $2.50)

210) Mr. Carlson needs to calculate 35% of 90. To do so, he uses the following equation: $\frac{35 \times 90}{100}$

Which of the following could he also have used?
A) (35 × 90) ÷ 100
B) (35 ÷ 90) × 100
C) (35 – 90) × 100
D) 90 × 0.0035

211) Item C costs 20% more per pound than item B. If a 12 pound container of item B costs $48, what is the cost per pound of item C?
   A) $4.12
   B) $4.20
   C) $4.60
   D) $4.80

212) The cost of a photography course is $20 per week plus a $5 fee per week for review of photographs and administration. What is the total cost of the course and fees for W weeks?
   A) $20W
   B) $25W
   C) $20 + 5W
   D) $5 + 20W

213) Which of the following shows the numbers ordered from least to greatest?
   A) $-1/4, 1/8, 1/6, 1$
   B) $-1/4, 1/8, 1, 1/6$
   C) $-1/4, 1/6, 1/8, 1$
   D) $-1/4, 1, 1/8, 1/6$

214) The graph below shows the relationship between the total number of hamburgers a restaurant sells and the total sales in dollars for the hamburgers. The cost of shakes, where c is the cost and s is the number of shakes, is represented by the following equation: $c = \frac{9}{4}s$. Which of the following best estimates difference between the cost of one hamburger and the cost of one shake?

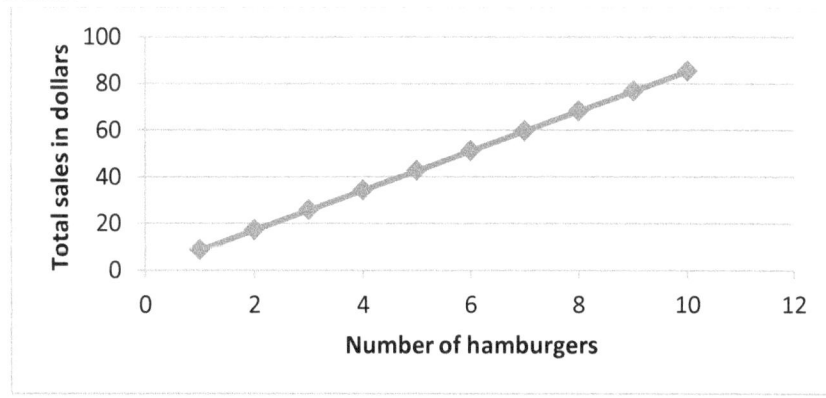

   A) $2.25
   B) $4.25
   C) $6.25
   D) $8.20

215) What is 12.86749 rounded to the nearest tenth?
   A) 10
   B) 12
   C) 12.8
   D) 12.9

216) You have spent $2/5$ of your operating budget at the end of 6 months of doing business. How much of your operating budget have you spent when expressed as a decimal number?
A) 0.20
B) 0.40
C) 0.45
D) 2.50

217) 4 out of every 5 employee-satisfaction questionnaires have been completed and returned. If a company has 250 total employees, and every employee must complete and return the questionnaire, how many questionnaires have not been completed and returned?
A) 4
B) 5
C) 50
D) 200

218) A store sells poinsettia plants for $20 during December and for $12 during January. In December, 55 customers purchased poinsettias, and 20 customers purchased them in January. How much money did the store receive for poinsettia sales during December and January?
A) $240
B) $1,060
C) $1,100
D) $1,340

219) A business prepares work orders to a strict time-budget system. Hours spent on a work order are recorded by the tenth of an hour in 6 minute increments. For a particular work order, $28^3/_{10}$ hours in total have been budgeted. Recording indicate that $7^9/_{10}$ hours on the work order. Which amount below represents the amount of time left for this work order?
A) $36^1/_5$
B) $35^6/_{10}$
C) $20^2/_5$
D) $20^3/_5$

220) A quarry mixes different kinds of decorative stone for customers to use for landscaping. For one type of decorative stone mix, 2 parts of white gravel must be used for every 3 parts of blue slate chippings. You have an order that requires 147 parts of blue slate chippings. How many parts of white gravel should be added?
A) 73.5
B) 88.0
C) 98.0
D) 220.5

221) Point B is at 0.35 on a number line and the distance between point B and point C is 1.2. Which of the following could be the location of point C?
   A) 0.23
   B) 0.47
   C) −0.85
   D) 0.85

222) What is the sum of 15.845 + 8.21 to the nearest integer?
   A) 24.055
   B) 24
   C) 23
   D) 22

223) Perform the operations: $(5x - 2)(3x^2 + 5x - 8)$
   A) $15x^3 + 19 + 50x + 16$
   B) $15x^3 + 19x^2 + 70x - 16$
   C) $15x^3 + 19x^2 - 50x + 16$
   D) $15x^3 + 19x^2 - 70x + 16$

224) Solve for x and y: $x + 5y = 24$ and $8x + 2y = 40$
   A) (4, 4)
   B) (−4, 4)
   C) (40, 4)
   D) (4, 38)

225) Perform the operation and express as one fraction: $\dfrac{2}{10x} + \dfrac{3}{12x^2}$
   A) $\dfrac{30x}{24x^2}$
   B) $\dfrac{5}{10x+12x^2}$
   C) $\dfrac{4x+5}{20x^2}$
   D) $\dfrac{24x^2}{30x}$

226) $\sqrt{50} + 4\sqrt{32} + 7\sqrt{2} = ?$
   A) $8\sqrt{58}$
   B) $28\sqrt{2}$
   C) $15\sqrt{58}$
   D) $16\sqrt{2}$

227) $10a^2b^3c \div 2ab^2c^2 = ?$
   A) $5c \div ab$
   B) $5a \div bc$
   C) $5ab \div c$
   D) $5ac \div b$

228) $\dfrac{\sqrt{48}}{3} + \dfrac{5\sqrt{5}}{6} = ?$
   A) $\dfrac{4\sqrt{3} + 5\sqrt{5}}{6}$
   B) $\dfrac{8\sqrt{3} + 5\sqrt{5}}{6}$
   C) $\dfrac{\sqrt{48} + 5\sqrt{5}}{9}$
   D) $\dfrac{6\sqrt{48} + 5\sqrt{5}}{18}$

229) What is the value of $\dfrac{x-3}{2-x}$ when $x = 1$?
   A) 2
   B) –2
   C) ½
   D) –½

230) $\sqrt[3]{5} \times \sqrt[3]{7} = ?$
   A) $\sqrt[3]{13}$
   B) $\sqrt[6]{13}$
   C) $\sqrt[9]{13}$
   D) $\sqrt[3]{35}$

231) If x and y are positive integers, the expression $\dfrac{1}{\sqrt{x} - \sqrt{y}}$ is equivalent to which of the following?
   A) $\sqrt{x} - y$
   B) $\sqrt{x} + y$
   C) $\dfrac{\sqrt{x} - y}{1}$
   D) $\dfrac{\sqrt{x} + \sqrt{y}}{x - y}$

232) If $x + y = 5$ and $a + b = 4$, what is the value of $(3x + 3y)(5a + 5b)$?
   A) 9
   B) 35
   C) 200
   D) 300

233) What are two possible values of x for the following equation? $x^2 + 6x + 8 = 0$
   A) 1 and 2
   B) 2 and 4
   C) 6 and 8
   D) −2 and −4

234) Which of the following mathematical expressions equals $^3/_{xy}$?
   A) $^3/_x \times {}^3/_y$
   B) $3 \div 3xy$
   C) $3 \div (xy)$
   D) $^1/_3 \div 3xy$

235) If $\frac{1}{5}x + 3 = 5$, then $x = ?$
   A) $\frac{8}{5}$
   B) $-\frac{8}{5}$
   C) 8
   D) 10

236) Solve for x: $x^2 - 12x + 35 < 0$
   A) 5 > x > 7
   B) 5 > x or x < 7
   C) 5 < x < 7
   D) 5 < x or x > 7

237) Which of the following expressions is equivalent to $2xy - 8x^2y + 6y^2x^2$?
   A) $2(xy - 4x^2y + 3x^2y^2)$
   B) $2xy(-4x + 3xy)$
   C) $2xy(1 - 4x + 3xy)$
   D) $2xy(1 + 4x - 3xy)$

238) A is 3 times B, and B is 3 more than 6 times C. Which of the following describes the relationship between A and C?
   A) A is 9 more than 18 times C.
   B) A is 3 more than 3 times C.
   C) A is 3 more than 18 times C.
   C) A is 6 more than 3 times C.

239) |6 − 13| = ?
   A) 19
   B) 7
   C) −7
   D) −19

240) Find the midpoint between the following coordinates: (5, 7) and (11, −3)
   A) (2, 5)
   B) (5, 2)
   C) (2, 8)
   D) (8, 2)

241) If $\sqrt{9z + 18} = 9$, then z = ?
   A) −1
   B) 6
   C) 7
   D) 63

242) If $z = \frac{x}{1-y}$, then y = ?
   A) $\frac{z}{x}$
   B) $\frac{x}{z} - 1$
   C) $-\frac{x}{z} + 1$
   D) $z - zx$

243) Perform the operation: $\sqrt{6} \cdot (\sqrt{40} + \sqrt{6})$
   A) $\sqrt{240} + \sqrt{6}$
   B) $\sqrt{46} + 6$
   C) 46
   D) $4\sqrt{15} + 6$

244) Which of the following is equivalent to $a^{½}b^{¼}c^{¾}$?
   A) $a^2bc^3 \div 4$
   B) $4(a^2bc^3)$
   C) $\sqrt{a} \times \sqrt[4]{b} \times \sqrt[4]{c^3}$
   D) $(ab^{¼}c^{¾} \div 2)$

245) $ab^8 \div ab^2$ = ?
   A) ab^6
   B) ab^4
   C) a^2b^6
   D) b^6

246) Martin is using a plaster mix to repair a wall in his house. The instructions for the mix state that 3 ounces of water should be added for every 4 ounces of plaster pounder used. If he uses 14 ounces of plaster powder, how much water should he add?
A) 56 ounces of water
B) 41 ounces of water
C) 10.5 ounces of water
D) 3 ounces of water

247) The graph below shows the cost in dollars of Item A as a function of the number of pounds purchased. The equation C = p × (7 ÷ 2) represents the cost of Item B, where p is the number of pounds and C is the cost. Which of the following statements best describes the relationship between the cost of Item A and the cost of Item B?

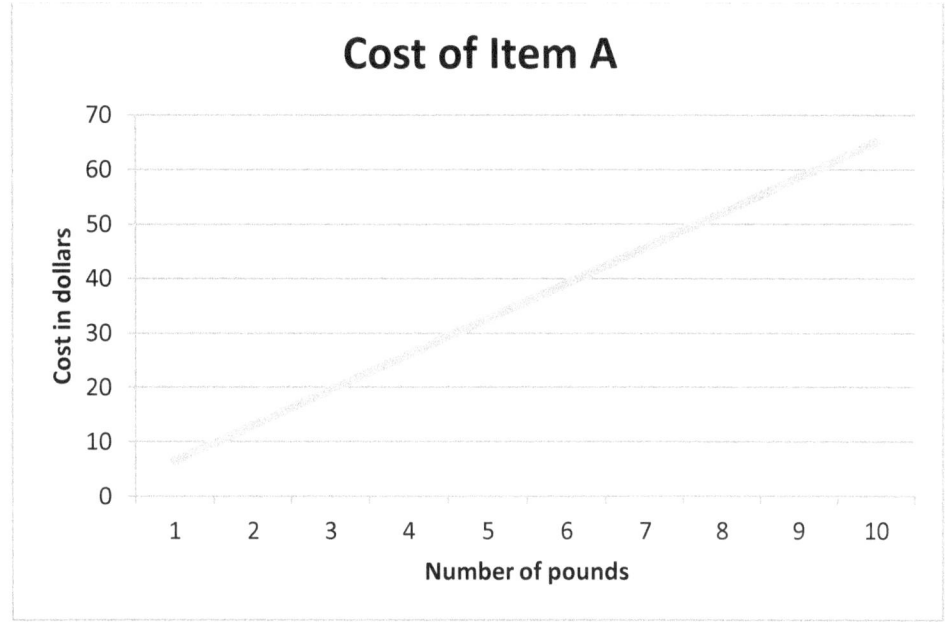

A) Item B costs $3.50 less per pound than Item A.
B) Item B costs $3.50 more per pound than Item A.
C) Item B costs $3 less per pound than Item A.
D) Item B costs $3 more per pound than Item A.

248) Perform the operation and express as one fraction: $\dfrac{1}{a+1} + \dfrac{1}{a}$

A) $\dfrac{2}{2a+1}$

B) $\dfrac{a+1}{a}$

C) $\dfrac{a^2+a}{2a+1}$

D) $\dfrac{2a+1}{a^2+a}$

249) For all $x \neq 0$ and $y \neq 0$, $\dfrac{5x}{1/xy} = ?$

   A) $\dfrac{5x}{xy}$

   B) $\dfrac{xy}{5x}$

   C) $\dfrac{5}{y}$

   D) $5x^2y$

250) You travel on a delivery route that has rest points marked out at equal intervals. There are 7 rest points on the route, including the rest point at your final destination. It takes $1^{1}/_{4}$ hours to travel to the first rest point. You are allowed a maximum 15 minute break at each rest point. If you travel at a constant speed, how much on-the-road time is needed, excluding time resting, in order to travel to your final destination?
   A) 7 hours and 15 minutes
   B) 7 hours and 45 minutes
   C) 8 hours and 45 minutes
   D) 10 hours

Solutions and Explanations for Practice Test Set 1 – Questions 1 to 80

1) The correct answer is D. Because two negatives make a positive, we know that – (–6) = 6. So, we can substitute this into the equation in order to solve it: – (–6) + 2 = 6 + 2 = 8

2) The correct answer is D. For problems that ask you to find the largest possible product of two even integers, first you need to divide the sum by 2. The sum in this problem is 30, so divide by 2: 30 ÷ 2 = 15. Now take the result from this division and find the 2 nearest even integers that are 1 number higher and lower: 15 + 1 = 16; 15 − 1 = 14. Finally, multiply these two numbers together in order to get the product: 16 × 14 = 224.

3) The correct answer is C. Multiply the numerators: 1 × 2 = 2. The multiply the denominators: 5 × 3 = 15. These numbers form the new fraction: $^2/_{15}$

4) The correct answer is B. Remember to invert the second fraction by putting the denominator on the top and the numerator on the bottom. So the second fraction $\frac{2}{3}$ becomes $\frac{3}{2}$ when inverted. Use the inverted fraction to solve the problem: $\frac{4}{7} \div \frac{2}{3} = \frac{4}{7} \times \frac{3}{2} = \frac{4 \times 3}{7 \times 2} = \frac{12}{14}$

5) The correct answer is A. Step 1 – To find the LCD, you have to look at the factors for each denominator. Factors are the numbers that equal a product when they are multiplied by each other. The factors of 8 are: 1 × **8** = 8; **2** × 4 = 8. The factors of 16 are: 1 × 16 = 16; **2** × **8** = 16; 4 × 4 = 16.
Step 2 – Determine which factors are common to both denominators by comparing the lists of factors. In this problem, the factors of 2 and 8 are common to the denominators of both fractions. (The numbers in bold above are the common factors.) Step 3 – Multiply the common factors to get the lowest common denominator. The numbers that are in bold above are then used to calculate the lowest common denominator: 2 × 8 = 16. Step 4 – Convert the denominator of each fraction to the LCD. You convert the fraction by referring to the factors from step 3. Multiply the numerator and the denominator by the same factor. We convert the first fraction as follows: $\frac{1}{8} \times \frac{2}{2} = \frac{2}{16}$. We do not need to convert the second

fraction because it already has the LCD. Step 5 – When both fractions have the same denominator, you can perform the operation to solve the problem: $\frac{2}{16} + \frac{3}{16} = \frac{5}{16}$

6) The correct answer is D. Step 1 – Look at the factors of the numerator and denominator. The factors of 12 are: 1 × 12 = 12; **2** × 6 = 12; 3 × 4 = 12. The factors of 14 are: 1 × 14 = 14; **2** × 7 = 14. So, we can see that the numerator and denominator have the common factor of 2. Step 2 – Simplify the fraction by dividing the numerator and denominator by the common factor. Simplify the numerator: 12 ÷ 2 = 6. Then simplify the denominator: 14 ÷ 2 = 7. Step 3 – Use the results from step 2 to form the new fraction. The numerator from step 2 is 6. The denominator is 7. So, the new fraction is $\frac{6}{7}$.

7) The correct answer is C. Step 1 – Convert the first mixed number to an integer plus a fraction. $4\frac{1}{8} = 4 + \frac{1}{8}$. Step 2 – Then multiply the integer by a fraction whose numerator and denominator are the same as the denominator of the existing fraction: $4 + \frac{1}{8} = \left(4 \times \frac{8}{8}\right) + \frac{1}{8} = \frac{4 \times 8}{8} + \frac{1}{8} = \frac{32}{8} + \frac{1}{8}$

Step 3 – Add the two fractions to get your new fraction: $\frac{32}{8} + \frac{1}{8} = \frac{33}{8}$. Then convert the second mixed number to a fraction, using the same steps that we have just completed for the first mixed number:

$3\frac{5}{6} = 3 + \frac{5}{6} = \left(3 \times \frac{6}{6}\right) + \frac{5}{6} = \frac{18}{6} + \frac{5}{6} = \frac{23}{6}$

Now that you have converted both mixed numbers to fractions, find the lowest common denominator and subtract to solve.

$\frac{33}{8} - \frac{23}{6} = \left(\frac{33}{8} \times \frac{3}{3}\right) - \left(\frac{23}{6} \times \frac{4}{4}\right) = \frac{(33 \times 3)}{(8 \times 3)} - \frac{(23 \times 4)}{(6 \times 4)} = \frac{99}{24} - \frac{92}{24} = \frac{99 - 92}{24} = \frac{7}{24}$

8) The correct answer is A. Do the multiplication and division from left to right. So, take the number to the left of the multiplication or division symbol and multiply or divide that number by the number on the right of the symbol. We need to multiply –5 by 4 and then divide 6 by 3.

You can see the order of operations more clearly if you put in parentheses to group the numbers together.

$-5 \times 4 - 6 \div 3 = (-5 \times 4) - (6 \div 3) = -20 - 2 = -22$

9) The correct answer is B. For this type of problem, do the operations inside the **parentheses** first.

$$\frac{4 \times (5-2)^3 + 6}{7 - 4 \div 2} = \frac{4 \times (3)^3 + 6}{7 - 4 \div 2}$$

Then do the operation on the **exponent**.

$$\frac{4 \times (3)^3 + 6}{7 - 4 \div 2} = \frac{4 \times 27 + 6}{7 - 4 \div 2}$$

Then do the **multiplication** and **division**.

$$\frac{4 \times 27 + 6}{7 - 4 \div 2} = \frac{(4 \times 27) + 6}{7 - (4 \div 2)} = \frac{108 + 6}{7 - 2}$$

Then do the **addition** and **subtraction**.

$$\frac{108 + 6}{7 - 2} = \frac{114}{5}$$

10) The correct answer is C. Determine the dollar amount of the reduction or discount:

$60 original price − $45 sale price = $15 discount. Then divide the discount by the original price to get the percentage of the discount: $15 ÷ $60 = 0.25 = 25%

11) The correct answer is B. The sales price of each item is five times the cost. The cost is expressed as B, so the sales price is 5B. The difference between the sales price of item and the cost of each item is the profit:

Sales Price − Cost = Profit

5B − B = 4B

12) The correct answer is D. The thousandths place is the third one to the right of the decimal. So, 0.96547 rounded to the nearest thousandth is 0.965.

13) The correct answer is B. Perform the division, and then check the decimal places of the numbers. Divide as follows: 1523.48 ÷ 100 = 15.2348. Reading our result from left to right: 1 is in the tens place, 5 is in the ones place, 2 is in the tenths place, 3 is in the hundredths place, 4 is in the thousandths place, and 8 is in the ten-thousandths place.

14) The correct answer is C. Determine which numbers can be calculated by multiplying another integer by 3: 1 × 3 = 3; 2 × 3 = 6; 3 × 3 = 9; and 4 × 3 = 12. 12 is greater than 11, so the nearest product to 11 from the list above is 9. Finally, we subtract these two numbers to get the remainder: 11 − 9 = 2

15) The correct answer is A. Line up the decimal points as shown when adding. Always remember to "carry the 1."

```
  1 1
  4.25
  0.003
  0.148
  4.401
```

16) The correct answer is A. From the facts in the problem, we know that η needs to be greater than $^{25}/_{13}$. If we convert $^{25}/_{13}$ to decimal form, we get 1.923077. The square root of 36 is 6, so (A) is the correct response because it is greater than 1.923077.

17) The correct answer is B. 7x is between 5 and 6, so set up an inequality as follows: $5 < 7x < 6$
Then insert the fractions from the answer choices for the value of x to solve the problem.

$5 < (7 \times {}^3/_4) < 6$

$5 < [(7 \times 3) \div 4] < 6$

$5 < (21 \div 4) < 6$

$5 < 5.25 < 6$

5.25 is between 5 and 6, so $^3/_4$ is the correct answer.

18) The correct answer is D. First of all, you need to determine the difference in temperature during the entire time period: 62 − 38 = 24 degrees less. Then calculate how much time has passed. From 5:00 PM

to 11:00 PM, 6 hours have passed. Next, divide the temperature difference by the amount of time that has passed to get the temperature change per hour: 24 degrees ÷ 6 hours = 4 degrees less per hour. To calculate the temperature at the stated time, you need to calculate the time difference. From 5:00 PM to 9:00 PM, 4 hours have passed. So, the temperature difference during the stated time is 4 hours × 4 degrees per hour = 16 degrees less. Finally, deduct this from the beginning temperature to get your final answer: 62° F – 16° F = 46° F.

19) The correct answer is C. For your first step, determine how many square feet there are in total: 2000 square feet per room × 8 rooms = 16,000 square feet in total. Then you need to divide by the coverage rate: 16,000 square feet to cover ÷ 900 square feet coverage per bucket = 17.77 buckets needed. It is not possible to purchase a partial bucket of paint, so 17.77 is rounded up to 18 buckets of paint.

20) The correct answer is D. Divide the distance traveled by the time in order to get the speed in miles per hour. Remember that in order to divide by a fraction, you need to invert the fraction, and then multiply. 3.6 miles ÷ $^3/_4$ = 3.6 × $^4/_3$ = (3.6 × 4) ÷ 3 = 14.4 ÷ 3 = 4.8 miles per hour

21) The correct answer is A. Multiply 25 times $15 to get the answer: 25 × $15 = $375

22) The correct answer is C. Each panel is 8 feet 6 inches long, and he needs 11 panels to cover the entire side of the field. So, we need to multiply 8 feet 6 inches by 11, and then simplify the result. Step 1 – 8 feet × 11 = 88 feet; Step 2 – 6 inches × 11 = 66 inches; Step 3 – There are 12 inches in a foot, so we need to determine how many feet and inches there are in 66 inches: 66 inches ÷ 12 = 5 feet 6 inches; Step 4 – Now add the two results together: 88 feet + 5 feet, 6 inches = 93 feet 6 inches

23) The correct answer is A. For problems with decimals, line the figures up in a column and add zeroes to fill in the column as shown below:

0.3500
0.0350
0.0530
0.3035

If you still struggle with decimals, you can remove the decimal points and the zeroes before the other integers in order to see the answer more clearly.

~~0.~~3500

~~0.0~~350

~~0.0~~530

~~0.~~3035

When we have removed the zeroes in front of the other numbers, we can clearly see that the largest number is 0.35.

24) The correct answer is D. The factors of 50 are: 1 × 50 = 50; 2 × 25 = 50; 5 × 10 = 50. If any of your factors are perfect squares, you can simplify the radical. 25 is a perfect square, so, you need to factor inside the radical sign as shown to solve the problem: $\sqrt{50} = \sqrt{25 \times 2} = \sqrt{5^2 \times 2} = \sqrt{5^2} \times \sqrt{2} = 5\sqrt{2}$

25) The correct answer is D. 36 is the common factor, So, factor the amounts inside the radicals and simplify: $\sqrt{36} + 4\sqrt{72} - 2\sqrt{144} = \sqrt{36} + 4\sqrt{36 \times 2} - 2\sqrt{36 \times 4} =$
$\sqrt{6 \times 6} + 4\sqrt{(6 \times 6) \times 2} - 2\sqrt{(6 \times 6) \times 4} = 6 + (4 \times 6)\sqrt{2} - (2 \times 6)\sqrt{4} =$
$6 + 24\sqrt{2} - (12 \times 2) = 6 + 24\sqrt{2} - 24 = -18 + 24\sqrt{2}$

26) The correct answer is A. $\sqrt{7} \times \sqrt{11} = \sqrt{7 \times 11} = \sqrt{77}$

27) The correct answer is B. The cube root is the number which satisfies the equation when multiplied by itself two times: $\sqrt[3]{\dfrac{216}{27}} = \sqrt[3]{\dfrac{6 \times 6 \times 6}{3 \times 3 \times 3}} = \dfrac{6}{3} = 2$

28) The correct answer is A. The base number is 7. Add the exponents: $7^5 \times 7^3 = 7^{(5+3)} = 7^8$

29) The correct answer is B. The base is xy. Subtract the exponents: $xy^6 \div xy^3 = xy^{(6-3)} = xy^3$

30) The correct answer is B. We have the base number of 10 and we are multiplying, so we can add the exponent of 5 to the exponent of −1: (1.7 × 10^5 miles per hour) × (2 × 10^{-1} hours) = 1.7 × 2 × $10^{(5 + -1)}$ = 3.4 × 10^4 = 3.4 × 10,000 = 34,000 miles

31) The correct answer is D. When you have a fraction as an exponent, the numerator is new exponent and the denominator goes in front as the root: $\sqrt{x^{\frac{5}{7}}} = \left(\sqrt[7]{x}\right)^5$

32) The correct answer is B. $x^{-5} = \dfrac{1}{x^5}$

33) The correct answer is C. We have a non-zero number raised to the power of zero, so it is equal to 1.

34) The correct answer is C.

$$\dfrac{b + \frac{2}{7}}{\frac{1}{b}} = \left(b + \dfrac{2}{7}\right) \div \dfrac{1}{b} = \left(b + \dfrac{2}{7}\right) \times \dfrac{b}{1} = b\left(b + \dfrac{2}{7}\right) = b^2 + \dfrac{2b}{7}$$

35) The correct answer is D. Find the lowest common denominator for the second fraction. Then add the numerators.

$$\dfrac{x^2}{x^2 + 2x} + \dfrac{8}{x} = \dfrac{x^2}{x^2 + 2x} + \left(\dfrac{8}{x} \times \dfrac{x + 2}{x + 2}\right) = \dfrac{x^2}{x^2 + 2x} + \dfrac{8x + 16}{x^2 + 2x} = \dfrac{x^2 + 8x + 16}{x^2 + 2x}$$

36) The correct answer is A. Multiply as shown: $\dfrac{2a^3}{7} \times \dfrac{3}{a^2} = \dfrac{2a^3 \times 3}{7 \times a^2} = \dfrac{6a^3}{7a^2}$

Then find the greatest common factor and cancel out to simplify: $\dfrac{6a^3}{7a^2} = \dfrac{6a \times a^2}{7 \times a^2} = \dfrac{6a \times \cancel{a^2}}{7 \times \cancel{a^2}} = \dfrac{6a}{7}$

37) The correct answer is B. Invert and multiply.

$$\dfrac{8x + 8}{x^4} \div \dfrac{5x + 5}{x^2} = \dfrac{8x + 8}{x^4} \times \dfrac{x^2}{5x+5} = \dfrac{(8x \times x^2) + (8 \times x^2)}{(x^4 \times 5x) + (x^4 \times 5)} = \dfrac{8x^3 + 8x^2}{5x^5 + 5x^4}$$

Then factor out (x + 1) from the numerator and denominator and cancel out:

$$\frac{8x^3 + 8x^2}{5x^5 + 5x^4} = \frac{(8x^2 \times x) + (8x^2 \times 1)}{(5x^4 \times x) + (5x^4 \times 1)} = \frac{8x^2(x+1)}{5x^4(x+1)} = \frac{8x^2 \cancel{(x+1)}}{5x^4 \cancel{(x+1)}} = \frac{8x^2}{5x^4}$$

Finally, factor out x^2 and cancel it out: $\frac{8x^2}{5x^4} = \frac{x^2 \times 8}{x^2 \times 5x^2} = \frac{\cancel{x^2} \times 8}{\cancel{x^2} \times 5x^2} = \frac{8}{5x^2}$

38) The correct answer is D. Use the FOIL method to expand the polynomial.

FIRST – Multiply the first term from the first set of parentheses by the first term from the second set of parentheses: (**x** + 4y)(**x** + 4y) = x × x = x^2

OUTSIDE – Multiply the first term from the first set of parentheses by the second term from the second set of parentheses: (**x** + 4y)(x + **4y**) = x × 4y = 4xy

INSIDE – Multiply the second term from the first set of parentheses by the first term from the second set of parentheses: (x + **4y**)(**x** + 4y) = 4y × x = 4xy

LAST– Multiply the second term from the first set of parentheses by the second term from the second set of parentheses: (x + **4y**)(x + **4y**) = 4y × 4y = $16y^2$

Finally, we add all of the products together: x^2 + 4xy + 4xy + $16y^2$ = x^2 + 8xy + $16y^2$

39) The correct answer is C. As the quantity of sugar increases, the amount of sleep also increases. A positive linear relationship therefore exists between the two variables. This is represented in chart C since the amount of sleep is greater when the amount of sugar consumed is higher.

40) The correct answer is C. We can see that the line does not begin on exactly on (5, 5), nor does it begin on (5, 9) because the first point is slightly below the horizontal line for y = 5. Therefore, we can rule out answers A and D. If we look at x = 20 on the graph, we can see that y = 18 at this point.

We can express this as the function: $f(x) = x \times 0.9$. Putting in the values of x from chart (C), we get the following: 5 × 0.9 = 4.5; 10 × 0.9 = 9; 15 × 0.9 =13.5; 20 × 0.9 = 18. This is represented in table C.

41) The correct answer is D. If a term or variable is subtracted within the parentheses, you have to keep the negative sign with it when you multiply.

FIRST: $(x - y)(x + y) = x \times x = x^2$

OUTSIDE: $(x - y)(x + y) = x \times y = xy$

INSIDE: $(x - y)(x + y) = -y \times x = -xy$

LAST: $(x - y)(x + y) = -y \times y = -y^2$

SOLUTION: $x^2 + xy + - xy - y^2 = x^2 - y^2$

42) The correct answer is A. First, Isolate the whole numbers.

$50 - \frac{3x}{5} \geq 41$

$(50 - 50) - \frac{3x}{5} \geq 41 - 50$

$-\frac{3x}{5} \geq -9$

Then get rid of the denominator on the fraction.

$-\frac{3x}{5} \geq -9$

$\left(5 \times -\frac{3x}{5}\right) \geq -9 \times 5$

$-3x \geq -9 \times 5$

$-3x \geq -45$

Then isolate the remaining whole numbers.

$-3x \geq -45$

$-3x \div 3 \geq -45 \div 3$

$-x \geq -45 \div 3$

$-x \geq -15$

Then deal with the negative number.

$-x \geq -15$

$-x + 15 \geq -15 + 15$

$-x + 15 \geq 0$

Finally, isolate the unknown variable as a positive number.

$-x + 15 \geq 0$

$-x + x + 15 \geq 0 + x$

$15 \geq x$

$x \leq 15$

43) The correct answer is D. Substitute values as shown: $x - 2 > 5$ and $y = x - 2$, so $y > 5$. If two wizfits are being purchased, we need to solve for $2y$:

$y \times 2 > 5 \times 2$

$2y > 10$

44) The correct answer is B. For quadratic inequality problems like this one, you need to factor the inequality first. The factors of -9 are: -1×9; -3×3; 1×-9. Because we do not have a term with only the x variable, we need factors that add up to zero, so factor as shown:

$x^2 - 9 < 0$

$(x + 3)(x - 3) < 0$

Then find values for x by solving each parenthetical for 0.

$(x + 3) = 0$

$(-3 + 3) = 0$

$x = -3$

$(x - 3) = 0$

$(3 - 3) = 0$

$x = 3$

So, $x > -3$ or $x < 3$

You can then check your work to be sure that you have the inequality signs pointing the right way.

Use -2 to check $x > -3$. Since $-2 > -3$ is correct, our proof should also be correct:

$x^2 - 9 < 0$

$-2^2 - 9 < 0$

$4 - 9 < 0$

−5 < 0 CORRECT

Use 4 to check for x < 3. Since 4 < 3 is incorrect, our proof should also be incorrect.

$x^2 - 9 < 0$

$4^2 - 9 < 0$

$16 - 9 < 0$

7 < 0 INCORRECT

Therefore, we have checked that x > −3 or x < 3.

45) The correct answer is D. We know that the products of 12 are: 1 × 12 = 12; 2 × 6 = 12; 3 × 4 = 12.

So, add each of the two factors together to solve the first equation: 1 + 12 = 13; 2 + 6 = 8; 3 + 4 = 7.

(3, 4) solves both equations, so it is the correct answer.

46) The correct answer is C. The first term of the second equation is x. To eliminate the x variable, we need to multiply the second equation by 3 because the first equation contains 3x.

$x + 2y = 8$

$(3 \times x) + (3 \times 2y) = (3 \times 8)$

$3x + 6y = 24$

Now subtract the new second equation from the original first equation.

$3x + 3y = 15$

$-(3x + 6y = 24)$

$-3y = -9$

Then solve for y.

$-3y = -9$

$-3y \div -3 = -9 \div -3$

$y = 3$

Using our original second equation of $x + 2y = 8$, substitute the value of 3 for y to solve for x.

$x + 2y = 8$

$x + (2 \times 3) = 8$

$x + 6 = 8$

$x + 6 - 6 = 8 - 6$

$x = 2$

47) The correct answer is B. First, find the midpoint of the x coordinates for (**−4**, 2) and (**8**,−6).

midpoint $x = (x_1 + x_2) \div 2$

midpoint $x = (-4 + 8) \div 2$

midpoint $x = 4 \div 2$

midpoint $x = 2$

Then find the midpoint of the y coordinates for (−4, **2**) and (8,**−6**).

midpoint $y = (y_1 + y_2) \div 2$

midpoint $y = (2 + -6) \div 2$

midpoint $y = -4 \div 2$

midpoint $y = -2$

So, the midpoint is (2, −2)

48) The correct answer is D. Substitute the values provided (2, 3) and (6, 7) into the formula.

$d = \sqrt{(x_2 - x_1)^2 + (y_2 - y_1)^2}$

$d = \sqrt{(6 - 2)^2 + (7 - 3)^2}$

$d = \sqrt{4^2 + 4^2}$

$d = \sqrt{16 + 16}$

$d = \sqrt{32}$

49) The correct answer is A. Substitute the values into the slope-intercept formula.

$y = mx + b$

$315 = m5 + 15$

$315 - 15 = m5 + 15 - 15$

$300 = m5$

$300 ÷ 5 = m5 ÷ 5$

$60 = m$

50) The correct answer is A. The x intercept is the point at which a line crosses the x axis of a graph. In order for the line to cross the x axis, y must be equal to zero at that particular point of the graph. On the other hand, the y intercept is the point at which the line crosses the y axis. So, in order for the line to cross the y axis, x must be equal to zero at that particular point of the graph. First, substitute 0 for y in order to find the x intercept.

$x^2 + 2y^2 = 144$

$x^2 + (2 × 0) = 144$

$x^2 + 0 = 144$

$x^2 = 144$

$x = 12$

Then substitute 0 for x in order to find the y intercept.

$x^2 + 2y^2 = 144$

$(0 × 0) + 2y^2 = 144$

$0 + 2y^2 = 144$

$2y^2 ÷ 2 = 144 ÷ 2$

$y^2 = 72$

$y = \sqrt{72}$

So, the y intercept is $(0, \sqrt{72})$ and the x intercept is $(12, 0)$.

Solutions and Explanations for Practice Test Set 2 – Questions 81 to 160

51) The correct answer is B. In our problem, if s% have been absent, then 100% − s% have not been absent. In other words, since a percentage is any given number out of 100%, the percentage of students who have not been absent is: (100% − s%). This equation is then multiplied by the total number of students (x) in order to determine the answer: (100% − s%) × x

52) The correct answer is B. Line up the numbers by the comma, and remember to carry the 1's:

```
  1 1 1
  1,594
+23,786
 25,380
```

53) The correct answer is A. This problem is like question 84 above, except here we need to find a missing value. Remember to put in zeroes and line up the decimal points when you compare the numbers.

   0.0007

A. 0.0012

B. 0.0006

C. 0.0022

D. 0.0220

   0.0021

Answer choice B is less than 0.0007, and answer choices C and D are greater than 0.0021. Answer choice A (0.0012) is between 0.0007 and 0.0021, so it is the correct answer.

54) The correct answer is A. The equation is: F = $500P + $3,700. We are told that the total funds are $40,000 so put that in the equation to solve the problem.

$40,000 = $500P + $3,700

$40,000 − $3,700 = $500P

$36,300 = $500P

$36,300 ÷ 500 = $500 ÷ 500P

$36,300 ÷ 500 = 72.6

Since a fraction of a project cannot be undertaken, the greatest number of projects is 72.

55) The correct answer is D. To answer this type of question, you need these principles: (a) Positive numbers are greater than negative numbers; (b) When two fractions have the same numerator, the fraction with the smaller number in the denominator is the larger fraction. Accordingly, 1 is greater than $1/5$; $1/5$ is greater than $1/7$, and $1/7$ is greater than $-1/3$.

56) The correct answer is A. The problem tells us that the morning flight had 52 passengers more than the evening flight, and there were 540 passengers in total on the two flights that day. Step 1 – First of all, we need to deduct the difference from the total: 540 – 52 = 488; In other words, there were 488 passengers on both flights combined, plus the 52 additional passengers on the morning flight.
Step 2 – Now divide this result by 2 to allocate an amount of passengers to each flight: 488 ÷ 2 = 244 passengers on the evening flight. (Had the question asked you for the amount of passengers on the morning flight, you would have had to add back the amount of additional passengers to find the total amount of passengers for the morning flight: 244 + 52 = 296 passengers on the morning flight)

57) The correct answer is C. Divide and then round up: 82 people in total ÷ 15 people served per container = 5.467 containers. We need to round up to 6 since we cannot purchase a fractional part of a container.

58) The correct answer is D. The question is asking us about a time duration of 6 minutes, so we need to calculate the amount of seconds in 6 minutes: 6 minutes × 60 seconds per minute = 360 seconds in total. Then divide the total time by the amount of time needed to make one journey: 360 seconds ÷ 45 seconds per journey = 8 journeys. Finally, multiply the number of journeys by the amount of inches per journey in order to get the total inches: 10.5 inches for 1 journey × 8 journeys = 84 inches in total

59) The correct answer is D. First of all, we need to find a common denominator for the fractions in the inequality, as well as for the fractions in the answer choices. In order to complete the problem quickly, you

should not try to find the lowest common denominator, but just find any common denominator. We can do this by expressing all of the numbers with a denominator of 90, since 9 is the largest denominator in the inequality and 10 is the largest denominator in the answer choices.

$2/3 \times 30/30 = 60/90$

$7/9 \times 10/10 = 70/90$

Then, express the original inequality in terms of the common denominator: $60/90 < ? < 70/90$

Next, convert the answer choices to the common denominator.

A) $1/3 \times 30/30 = 30/90$

B) $1/5 \times 18/18 = 18/90$

C) $2/6 \times 15/15 = 30/90$

D) $7/10 \times 9/9 = 63/90$

Finally, compare the results to find the answer. By comparing the numerators, we can see that $63/90$ lies between $60/90$ and $70/90$. So, D is the correct answer because $60/90 < 63/90 < 70/90$.

60) The correct answer is C. If $\frac{x}{24}$ is between 8 and 9, x will need to be between 192 and 216, since $\frac{192}{24} = 192 \div 24 = 8$ and $\frac{216}{24} = 216 \div 24 = 9$. 200 is the only number from the answer choices that is greater than 192 and less than 216.

61) The correct answer is C. Work backwards based on the facts given. There are 18 students left at the end after one-fourth of them left for the principal's office. So, set up an equation for this:

$18 + 1/4 T = T$

$18 + 1/4 T - 1/4 T = T - 1/4 T$

$18 = 3/4 T$

$18 \times 4 = 3/4 T \times 4$

$72 = 3T$

$72 \div 3 = 3T \div 3$

$24 = T$

So, before the group of pupils left to see the principal, there were 24 students in the class. We know that one-fifth of the students left at the beginning to go to singing lessons, so we need to set up an equation for this:

$24 + \frac{1}{5}T = T$

$24 + \frac{1}{5}T - \frac{1}{5}T = T - \frac{1}{5}T$

$24 = \frac{4}{5}T$

$24 \times 5 = \frac{4}{5}T \times 5$

$120 = 4T$

$120 \div 4 = 4T \div 4$

$30 = T$

62) The correct answer is B. At the beginning of January, there are 300 students, but 5% of the students leave during the month, so we have 95% left at the end of the month: 300 × 95% = 285. Then 15 students join on the last day of the month, so we add that back in to get to the total at the end of January: 285 + 15 = 300. If this pattern continues, there will always be 300 students in the academy at the end of any month.

63) The correct answer is D. Calculate the discount: $120 × 12.5% = $15 discount. Then subtract the discount from the original price to determine the sales price: $120 − $15 = $105

64) The correct answer is C. Divide by the fractional hour in order to determine the speed for an entire hour: 38.4 miles ÷ $\frac{4}{5}$ of an hour = 38.4 × $\frac{5}{4}$ = (38 × 5) ÷ 4 = 47.5 mph. We round this up to 48 mph.

65) The correct answer is A. The ratio of defective chips to functioning chips is 1 to 20. So, the defective chips form one group and the functioning chips form another group. Therefore, the total data set can be divided into groups of 21. Accordingly, $\frac{1}{21}$ of the chips will be defective. The factory produced 11,235 chips last week, so we calculate as follows: 11,235 × $\frac{1}{21}$ = 535

66) The correct answer is B. Add the three figures together to solve: 75.25 + 10.75 + 3.20 = 89.2

67) The correct answer is A. Add the percentages together to solve: 45% + 35% = 80%

68) The correct answer is D. Step 1 – Convert the mixed number to a decimal: $2\frac{1}{2}$ = 2.5 hours. Step 2 – Multiply this result by the number of units: 2.5 hours per unit × 5 units = 12.5 hours. Step 3 – Convert the decimal to minutes: 0.5 hour = 30 minutes. Step 4 – Express your answer in hours and minutes: 12 hours and 30 minutes

69) The correct answer is C. When determining how much has been sold, you are most likely start the calculation with the amount in stock at the beginning of the month. You would begin the calculation with the 105 pens at the start of the month, then add the 400 pens purchased, and then subtract the 350 pens left to find out how many pens you have sold.

70) The correct answer is D. Step 1 – Calculate the total amount of miles for the white lines for six years. There is a double white line, so we have to multiply by 2: 500 × 2 = 1,000 miles. Step 2 – Add in the amount for the yellow line = 1,000 + 200 = 1,200 miles total for six years. Step 3 – Double the result from the previous step to get the amount for 12 years: 1,200 × 2 = 2,400

71) The correct answer is B. The total amount available is $55,000, so we can substitute this for C in the equation provided in order to calculate R number of residents:

C = $750R + $2,550

$55,000 = $750R + $2,550

$55,000 – $2,550 = $750R + $2,550 – $2,550

$55,000 – $2,550 = $750R

$52,450 = $750R

$52,450 ÷ $750 = $750R ÷ $750

$52,450 ÷ $750 = R

69.9 = R

It is not possible to accommodate a fractional part of one person, so we need to round down to 69 residents.

72) The correct answer is B.

Factor: $x^2 - 5x + 6 \leq 0$

$(x - 2)(x - 3) \leq 0$

Then solve each parenthetical for zero:

$(x - 2) = 0$

$2 - 2 = 0$

$x = 2$

$(x - 3) = 0$

$3 - 3 = 0$

$x = 3$

So, $2 \leq x \leq 3$

Now check. Use 1 to check to $2 \leq x$, which is the same as $x \geq 2$. Since 1 is not actually greater than or equal to 2, our proof for this should be incorrect.

$x^2 - 5x + 6 \leq 0$

$1^2 - (5 \times 1) + 6 \leq 0$

$1 - 5 + 6 \leq 0$

$-4 + 6 \leq 0$

$2 \leq 0$ INCORRECT

Use 2.5 to check for $x \leq 3$. Since 2.5 really is less than 3, our proof should be correct.

$x^2 - 5x + 6 \leq 0$

$2.5^2 - (5 \times 2.5) + 6 \leq 0$

$6.25 - 12.5 + 6 \leq 0$

$-0.25 \leq 0$ CORRECT

Therefore, we have checked that $2 \leq x \leq 3$

73) The correct answer is B. Substitute 12 for the value of x. Then simplify and solve.

$x^2 + xy - y = 254$

$12^2 + 12y - y = 254$

$144 + 12y - y = 254$

$144 - 144 + 12y - y = 254 - 144$

$12y - y = 110$

$11y = 110$

$11y \div 11 = 110 \div 11$

$y = 10$

74) The correct answer is A.

FIRST: $(\mathbf{3x} + y)(\mathbf{x} - 5y) = 3x \times x = 3x^2$

OUTSIDE: $(\mathbf{3x} + y)(x - \mathbf{5y}) = 3x \times -5y = -15xy$

INSIDE: $(3x + \mathbf{y})(\mathbf{x} - 5y) = y \times x = xy$

LAST: $(3x + \mathbf{y})(x - \mathbf{5y}) = y \times -5y = -5y^2$

Then add all of the above once you have completed FOIL: $3x^2 - 15xy + xy - 5y^2 = 3x^2 - 14xy - 5y^2$

75) The correct answer is A. The factors of 9 are: $1 \times 9 = 9$; $\mathbf{3} \times \mathbf{3} = 9$. The factors of 3 are: $1 \times \mathbf{3} = 3$.

So, put the integer for the common factor outside the parentheses first: $9x^3 - 3x = 3(3x^3 - x)$

Then determine if there are any common variables for the terms that remain in the parentheses.

For $(3x^2 - x)$ the terms $3x^2$ and x have the variable x in common. So, now factor out x to solve:

$3(3x^3 - x) = 3x(3x^2 - 1)$

76) The correct answer is A. As y increases by 5, x decreases by 5. So, the slope is –1. The line includes point (20, 15), which is the fifth point from the left.

77) The correct answer is B. Add the numbers in front of the radical signs to solve. If there is no number before the radical, then put in the number 1 because then the radical will count only 1 time when you add.

$\sqrt{15} + 3\sqrt{15} = 1\sqrt{15} + 3\sqrt{15} = (1 + 3)\sqrt{15} = 4\sqrt{15}$

78) The correct answer is C. In order to multiply two square roots, multiply the numbers inside the radical signs: $\sqrt{5} \times \sqrt{3} = \sqrt{5 \times 3} = \sqrt{15}$

79) The correct answer is B. Find the lowest common denominator. Then add the numerators together as shown: $\frac{x}{5} + \frac{y}{2} = \left(\frac{x}{5} \times \frac{2}{2}\right) + \left(\frac{y}{2} \times \frac{5}{5}\right) = \frac{2x}{10} + \frac{5y}{10} = \frac{2x + 5y}{10}$

80) The correct answer is D. The slope intercept formula is: $y = mx + b$. Remember that m is the slope and b is the y intercept. You will also need the slope formula: $m = \frac{y_2 - y_1}{x_2 - x_1}$

We are given the slope, as well as point (4,5), so first we need to put those points into the slope formula. We are doing this in order to solve for b, which is not provided in the facts of the problem.

$$\frac{y_2 - y_1}{x_2 - x_1} = -\frac{3}{5}$$

$$\frac{5 - y_1}{4 - x_1} = -\frac{3}{5}$$

Then eliminate the denominator.

$$(4 - x_1)\frac{5 - y_1}{4 - x_1} = -\frac{3}{5}(4 - x_1)$$

$$5 - y_1 = -\frac{3}{5}(4 - x_1)$$

Now put in 0 for x_1 in the slope formula in order to find b, which is the y intercept (the point at which the line crosses the y axis).

$$5 - y_1 = -\frac{3}{5}(4 - x_1)$$

$$5 - y_1 = -\frac{3}{5}(4 - 0)$$

$$5 - y_1 = -\frac{3 \times 4}{5}$$

$$5 - y_1 = -\frac{12}{5}$$

$$5 - 5 - y_1 = -\frac{12}{5} - 5$$

$$-y_1 = -\frac{12}{5} - 5$$

$$-y_1 \times -1 = \left(-\frac{12}{5} - 5\right) \times -1$$

$$y_1 = \frac{12}{5} + 5$$

$$y_1 = \frac{12}{5} + \left(5 \times \frac{5}{5}\right)$$

$$y_1 = \frac{12}{5} + \frac{25}{5}$$

$$y_1 = \frac{37}{5}$$

Remember that the *y* intercept (known in the slope-intercept formula as the variable *b*) exists when *x* is equal to 0. We have put in the value of 0 for *x* in the equation above, so $b = \frac{37}{5}$. Now put the value for *b* into the slope intercept formula.

$$y = mx + b$$

$$y = -\frac{3}{5}x + \frac{37}{5}$$

81) The correct answer is D. Factor and cancel out if possible. Then multiply.

$$\frac{x^2 + 5x + 4}{x^2 + 6x + 5} \times \frac{16}{x + 5} =$$

$$\frac{(x+1)(x+4)}{(x+1)(x+5)} \times \frac{16}{x+5} =$$

$$\frac{\cancel{(x+1)}(x+4)}{\cancel{(x+1)}(x+5)} \times \frac{16}{x+5} =$$

$$\frac{(x+4)}{(x+5)} \times \frac{16}{x+5} =$$

$$\frac{(x+4) \times 16}{(x+5)(x+5)} =$$

$$\frac{16x + 64}{x^2 + 10x + 25}$$

82) The correct answer is D. When dividing fractions, you need to invert the second fraction and then multiply the two fractions together.

$$\frac{8x-8}{x} \div \frac{3x-3}{6x^2} = \frac{8x-8}{x} \times \frac{6x^2}{3x-3}$$

Then look at the numerator and denominator from the result of the previous step to see if you can factor and cancel out.

$$\frac{8x-8}{x} \times \frac{6x^2}{3x-3} =$$

$$\frac{8(x-1)}{x} \times \frac{6x^2}{3(x-1)} =$$

$$\frac{8\cancel{(x-1)}}{x} \times \frac{6x^2}{3\cancel{(x-1)}} =$$

$$\frac{8 \times 6x^2}{x \times 3} =$$

$$\frac{8 \times (2 \times 3 \times x \times x)}{x \times 3} =$$

$$\frac{8 \times (2 \times \cancel{3} \times \cancel{x} \times x)}{\cancel{x \times 3}} = 16x$$

83) The correct answer is C. Any non-zero number to the power of zero is equal to 1.

84) The correct answer is B. $4^{11} \times 4^8 = 4^{(11+8)} = 4^{19}$

85) The correct answer is C. Perform the operation on the radicals and then simplify.

$$\sqrt{8x^4} \cdot \sqrt{32x^6} = \sqrt{8x^4 \times 32x^6} = \sqrt{256x^{10}} = \sqrt{16 \times 16 \times x^5 \times x^5} = 16x^5$$

86) The correct answer is A. Remember that the y intercept is where the line crosses the y axis, so x = 0 for the y intercept. Begin by substituting 0 for x.

y = x + 14

y = 0 + 14

y = 14

Therefore, the coordinates (0, 14) represent the y intercept.

On the other hand, the x intercept exists where the line crosses the x axis, so y = 0 for the x intercept.

Now substitute 0 for y.

y = x + 14

0 = x + 14

0 – 14 = x + 14 – 14

–14 = x

So, the coordinates (–14, 0) represent the x intercept.

87) The correct answer is A. Our points are (5, 2) and (7, 4), so substitute the values into the midpoint formula.

$(x_1 + x_2) \div 2 , (y_1 + y_2) \div 2$

(5 + 7) ÷ 2 = midpoint x, (2 + 4) ÷ 2 = midpoint y

12 ÷ 2 = midpoint x, 6 ÷ 2 = midpoint y

6 = midpoint x, 3 = midpoint y

88) The correct answer is C. The plumber is going to earn $4,000 for the month. He charges a set fee of $100 per job, and he will do 5 jobs, so we can calculate the total set fees first: $100 set fee per job × 5 jobs = $500 total set fees. Then deduct the set fees from the total for the month in order to determine the total for the hourly pay: $4,000 – $500 = $3,500. He earns $25 per hour, so divide the hourly rate into the total hourly pay in order to determine the number of hours he will work: $3,500 total hourly pay ÷ $25 per hour = 140 hours to work

89) The correct answer is D. $(2 + \sqrt{6})^2 = (2 + \sqrt{6})(2 + \sqrt{6}) =$

$(2 \times 2) + (2 \times \sqrt{6}) + (2 \times \sqrt{6}) + (\sqrt{6} \times \sqrt{6}) = 4 + 4\sqrt{6} + 6 = 10 + 4\sqrt{6}$

90) The correct answer is D. Using the slope formula, we can calculate the slope of the line as follows:

$\frac{y_2 - y_1}{x_2 - x_1} = \frac{8 - 4}{6 - 0} = \frac{4}{6} = \frac{2}{3}$. So, variable m for the slope needs to be $\frac{2}{3}$ for our equation. The line crosses the *y* axis at point (0, 4), so the *y* intercept is 4. Finally, put these values into the equation of a line to solve: $y = \frac{2}{3}x + 4$

91) The correct answer is C. Before we shift the figure, point C has the coordinates (–4, –3). We are moving the figure 7 units to the right, thereby adding 7 to the *x* coordinate, and 6 units down, thereby subtracting 6 from the *y* coordinate. –4 + 7 = 3 and –3 – 6 = –9, so the new coordinates are: (3, –9).

92) The correct answer is C. The *y* intercept is where *x* = 0. So, we can substitute 0 in our equation to solve: ($12 + $2*x*) ÷ (4 + *x*) = ($12 + 0) ÷ (4 + 0) = $12 ÷ 4 = 3.

93) The correct answer is A. The total amount that Toby has to pay is represented by C. He is paying D dollars immediately, so we can determine the remaining amount that he owes by deducting his down payment from the total. So, the remaining amount owing is represented by the equation: C – D. We have to divide the remaining amount owing by the number of months (M) to get the monthly payment (P):

P = (C – D) ÷ M = $\frac{C-D}{M}$

94) The correct answer is B. Assign a variable for the age of each brother. Alex = A, Burt = B, and Zander = Z. Alex is twice as old as Burt, so A = 2B. Burt is one year older than three times the age of Zander, so B = 3Z + 1. Then substitute the value of B into the first equation.

A = 2B

A = 2(3Z + 1)

A = 6Z + 2

So, Alex is 2 years older than 6 times the age of Zander.

95) The correct answer is D. The original price of the sofa on Wednesday was *x*. On Thursday, the sofa was reduced by 10%, so the price on Thursday was 90% of *x* or 0.90*x*. On Friday, the sofa was reduced by a further 15%, so the price on Friday was 85% of the price on Thursday, so we can multiply Thursday's price by 0.85 to get our answer: (0.90)(0.85)*x*

96) The correct answer is C. Step 1 – Determine the cost from the first supplier: 350 × 0.85 = $297.50. The tax on this will be $297.50 × 8.5% = $25.29. Then add the tax to the cost to get the total for the first supplier: $297.50 + $25.29 = $322.79. Step 2 – Then determine the total cost from the second supplier: $295 cost + ($295 × 0.085 tax) = $295 + 25.08 = $320.08. So, you will get the better deal from the second supplier at $320.08.

97) The correct answer is D. To calculate a reverse percentage you need to divide, rather than multiply. So, take the $123 discount and divide by the 40% percentage: $123 ÷ 40% = $123 ÷ 0.40 = $307.50

98) The correct answer is A. Step 1 – Find the total weight of the product by subtracting the weight of the empty crate. The crate weighs 90 pounds and 12 ounces when it contains the product and 15 pounds when it is empty, so the product itself weighs: 90 pounds and 12 ounces – 15 pounds = 75 pounds and 12 ounces. Step 2 – Use the formula from the formula sheet to convert the total weight of the product from pounds and ounces to just ounces. 1 pound = 16 ounces, so 75 pounds and 12 ounces = (75 × 16) + 12 = 1200 + 12 = 1212 ounces. Step 3 – The problem tells us that each can of tomato sauce weighs 12 ounces. Take the total weight from the previous step and divide by the weight per unit to determine how many units the crate contains: 1212 ounces ÷ 12 ounces per unit = 101 units

99) The correct answer is B. 1 foot = 0.3048 meters, so to convert to meters we need to multiply feet by 0.3048. 1 meter = 1,000 millimeters, so to convert from meters to millimeters, we need to multiply again by 1,000. So, the correct formula is as follows: millimeters = feet × 0.3048 × 1,000

100) The correct answer is A. In this problem, the measurements are taken in square yards. We can see from our formula sheet that 1 square yard = 9 square feet. The formula converts yards to feet, so we need to multiply square yards by 9 to convert to square feet. We can also see from the formula sheet that 1 acre = 43,560 square feet. However, this formula converts acres to square feet (rather than square feet to acres) so we need to divide the result from the previous step by 43,560 to calculate the acres. So, the correct formula is as follows: acres = (square yards × 9) ÷ 43,560

Solutions and Explanations for Practice Test Set 3 – Questions 161 to 240

101) The correct answer is C. The value of µ must be greater than $^{11}/_3$, which is equal to 3.6667. The answer 4.1 is the only option which meets this criterion.

102) The correct answer is C. Remember that the order of operations is PEMDAS: Parentheses, Exponents, Multiplication, Division, Addition, and Subtraction. There are no operations with parentheses, exponents, or multiplication. So, do the division first: 9 ÷ 3 = 3. Then replace this in the equation: 82 + 9 ÷ 3 – 5 = 82 + 3 – 5 = 80

103) The correct answer is A. This is another problem on the order of operations. There are no operations with parentheses or exponents, so do the multiplication first: 6 × 3 = 18. Then put this number in the equation: 52 + 6 × 3 – 48 = 52 + 18 – 48 = 22

104) The correct answer is C. In order to convert a fraction to a decimal, you must divide.

```
     .25
16)4.00
   3.2
   0.80
   0.80
      0
```

105) The correct answer is D. 30 percent in decimal form equals to 0.30. The phrase "of what number" shows that we have to divide: 90 ÷ 0.30 = 300. We can check this result as follows. 300 × 0.30 = 90.

106) The correct answer is A. Questions like this test your knowledge of mixed numbers. Mixed numbers are those that contain a whole number and a fraction. If the fraction on the first mixed number is greater than the fraction on the second mixed number, you can subtract the whole numbers and the fractions separately. Remember to use the lowest common denominator on the fractions. First, subtract whole numbers: 6 – 2 = 4

Then subtract fractions.

$^3/_4 - ^1/_2 =$

$^3/_4 - {}^2/_4 =$

$^1/_4$

Now put them together for the result.

4 ¼

107) The correct answer is D. Remember PEMDAS: Parentheses, Exponents, Multiplication, Division, Addition, and Subtraction. So, you must do the division and multiplication first, before adding or subtracting: $9 \times 6 + 42 \div 6 = (9 \times 6) + (42 \div 6)$. We know that $9 \times 6 = 54$ and $42 \div 6 = 7$ so perform the operations and simplify: $(9 \times 6) + (42 \div 6) = 54 + 7 = 61$.

108) The correct answer is B. To find the total amount contributed, you need to multiply.

31 × 12 = 372

109) The correct answer is D. When you are asked to divide fractions, remember that you need to invert the second fraction. Then you multiply this inverted fraction by the first fraction given in the problem. $^4/_3$ inverted is $^3/_4$. Then multiply the numerators and the denominators together to get the new fraction.

$$\frac{1}{8} \div \frac{4}{3} = \frac{1}{8} \times \frac{3}{4} = \frac{3}{32}$$

110) The correct answer is D. Convert the fractions in the mixed numbers to decimals.

$^3/_4 = 3 \div 4 = 0.75$

$^1/_5 = 1 \div 5 = 0.20$

Then represent the mixed numbers as decimal numbers.

Person 1: $14^3/_4 = 14.75$; Person 2: $20^1/_5 = 20.20$; Person 3: 36.35

Then add all three amounts together to find the total: 14.75 + 20.20 + 36.35 = 71.30

111) The correct answer is C. Remember that to represent a fraction as a decimal, you need to divide. So, you will need to do long division to determine the answer.

```
      .10
50)5.00
    5.00
       0
```

112) The correct answer is D. Be careful not to confuse remainders with decimals. The remainder is the whole number amount left over after you have used whole numbers to divide.

```
     66
9)600
   54
   60
   54
    6 – This is the remainder.
```

113) The correct answer is A. This question assesses your knowledge of mixed numbers. In this problem, the fraction on the second number is bigger than the fraction on the first number. So, we have to convert the mixed numbers to fractions first.

$$3\frac{1}{2} - 2\frac{3}{5} = \left[\left(3 \times \frac{2}{2}\right) + \frac{1}{2}\right] - \left[\left(2 \times \frac{5}{5}\right) + \frac{3}{5}\right] = \left[\frac{6}{2} + \frac{1}{2}\right] - \left[\frac{10}{5} + \frac{3}{5}\right] = \frac{7}{2} - \frac{13}{5} =$$

Then find the lowest common denominator.

$$\frac{7}{2} - \frac{13}{5} = \left(\frac{7}{2} \times \frac{5}{5}\right) - \left(\frac{13}{5} \times \frac{2}{2}\right) = \frac{35}{10} - \frac{26}{10} = \frac{9}{10}$$

114) The correct answer is B. Step 1 – Calculate the average high temperature in Fahrenheit. To do so, find the total for all five days and divide the result by 5: (72 + 68 + 65 + 82 + 81) ÷ 5 = 368 ÷ 5 = 73.6°F average. Step 2 – Covert the average in Fahrenheit to Celsius using the formula from the formula sheet. To convert Fahrenheit to Celsius, we use this formula: °C = 0.56(°F – 32) = 0.56(73.6° – 32) = 0.56(41.6) = 0.56 × 41.6 = 23.296, which we round to 23°C.

115) The correct answer is D. Step 1 – Determine the rate for the manicures: 5 hours ÷ 4 manicures = 1.25 hours per manicure = 1 hour and 15 minutes per manicure. Step 2 – Calculate the time needed for all 20 manicures: 1.25 hours per manicure × 20 manicures = 25 hours. Step 3 – Determine the rate for

the pedicures: 2.5 hours ÷ 5 pedicures = 0.5 hours per pedicure. Step 4 – Calculate the time needed to do all 25 pedicures: 0.5 hours × 25 pedicures = 12.5 hours = 12 hours and 30 minutes per pedicure. Step 5 – Find the total for all of the manicures and pedicures: 25 hours + 12.5 hours = 37.5 hours = 37 hours and 30 minutes

116) The correct answer is C. Step 1 – Calculate the daily rate in terms of a daily percentage: 57.75% ÷ 7 days = 8.25% per day. Step 2 – Divide this amount into 100% to find the approximate number of days in total: 100% ÷ 8.25% per day = 12.12 days, which we round down to 12 days.

117) The correct answer is C. Step 1 – Determine the cost for the first supplier: 135 units × $15.30 per unit = $2,065.50. The tax on this is: $2,065.50 × 0.06 = $123.93, so the total cost is: $2,065.50 + $123.93 = $2189.43. Step 2 – The total cost for the other supplier is: $2,100 + 75 = $2,175. So, you will get the best price from the second company.

118) The correct answer is B. Remember for division of fractions, you need to invert the second fraction and then multiply the fractions. When you multiply fractions, you multiply the numerators with each other for the new numerator, and the denominators with each other for the new denominator. For problems like this, deal with the parts of the equation in the parentheses first.

$$\frac{1}{6}+\left(\frac{1}{2}\div\frac{3}{8}\right)-\left(\frac{1}{3}\times\frac{3}{2}\right)=\frac{1}{6}+\left(\frac{1}{2}\times\frac{8}{3}\right)-\left(\frac{1}{3}\times\frac{3}{2}\right)=\frac{1}{6}+\frac{8}{6}-\frac{3}{6}$$

After you have done the operations on the parentheses, you can add and subtract as needed.

$$\frac{1}{6}+\frac{8}{6}-\frac{3}{6}=\frac{9}{6}-\frac{3}{6}=\frac{6}{6}=1$$

119) The correct answer is D. We know that Mary has already gotten 80% of the money. However, the question is asking how much money she still needs: 100% − 80% = 20% = .20

Now do the multiplication: 650 × .20 = 130

120) The correct answer is B. Your equation is: (A × $5) + (B × $8) = $60. They buy 4 of product A, so put that in the equation and solve it.

(A × $5) + (B × $8) = $60

(4 × $5) + (B × $8) = $60

$20 + (B × $8) = $60

(B × $8) = $40

B = 5

121) The correct answer is D. For practical problems like this, you must first determine the percentage that you need in order to solve the problem. Then, you must do long multiplication to determine how many games the team won. The question tells you the percentage of games the team lost, not won.

Step 1 – First of all, we have to calculate the percentage of games won. If the team lost 20 percent of the games, we know that the team won the remaining 80 percent.

Step 2 – Now do the long multiplication.

```
   50  games in total
 ×.80  percentage of games won (in decimal form)
 40.0  total games won
```

122) The correct answer is B. Step 1 – Look to see what information is common to both the question and to the information provided. Here we have the information that he can run 3 miles in 25 minutes. The question is asking how long it will take him to run 12 miles, so the commonality is miles. Step 2 – Next, you need to find out how many 3-mile increments there are in 12 miles: 12 ÷ 3 = 4. Step 3 – Then you need to determine the time required to travel the stated distance. Accordingly, we need to multiply the time for 3 miles by 4: 25 minutes × 4 = 100. So, 100 minutes are needed to run 12 miles. Step 4 – Finally, simplify into hours and minutes based on the fact that there are 60 minutes in one hour: 100 minutes = 1 hour 40 minutes.

123) The correct answer is A. Step 1 – First of all, we need to find out how many pieces of candy there are in total: 43 + 28 + 31 = 102 total pieces of candy. Step 2 – We need to divide the total amount of

candy by the number of students in order to find out how much candy each student will get: 102 total pieces of candy ÷ 34 students = 3 pieces of candy per student.

124) The correct answer is D. The lowest temperature is –10°F, and the highest temperature is 13°F. The difference between these two figures is calculated by subtracting. Be careful when you subtract. In particular, remember that when you see two negative signs together, you need to add. In other words, two negatives make a positive: 13 – (–10) = 13 + 10 = 23

125) The correct answer is A. Expand by multiplying the terms as shown below:

FIRST: (**x** – 5)(**3x** + 8) = $x \times 3x = 3x^2$

OUTSIDE: (**x** – 5)(3x + **8**) = $x \times 8 = 8x$

INSIDE: (x – **5**)(**3x** + 8) = $-5 \times 3x = -15x$

LAST: (x – **5**)(3x + **8**) = $-5 \times 8 = -40$

Then add all of the individual results together: $3x^2 + 8x + -15x + -40 = 3x^2 - 7x - 40$

126) The correct answer is C. Isolate the integers to one side of the equation.

$$\frac{3}{4}x - 2 = 4$$

$$\frac{3}{4}x - 2 + 2 = 4 + 2$$

$$\frac{3}{4}x = 6$$

Then get rid of the fraction by multiplying both sides by the denominator.

$$\frac{3}{4}x \times 4 = 6 \times 4$$

$$3x = 24$$

Then divide to solve the problem.

$$3x \div 3 = 24 \div 3$$

$$x = 8$$

127) The correct answer is D.

Factor: $x^2 + 2x - 8 \leq 0$

$(x + 4)(x - 2) \leq 0$

Then solve each parenthetical for zero:

$(x + 4) = 0$

$-4 + 4 = 0$

$x = -4$

$(x - 2) = 0$

$2 - 2 = 0$

$x = 2$

So our solution is, $-4 \leq x \leq 2$

Now check. Use 0 to check to for $x \leq 2$. Since 0 is actually less than 2, our proof for this should be correct.

$x^2 + 2x - 8 \leq 0$

$0 + 0 - 8 \leq 0$

$-8 \leq 0$ CORRECT

Use -5 to check for $-4 \leq x$. Since $-4 \leq -5$ is incorrect, our proof should also be incorrect.

$x^2 + 2x - 8 \leq 0$

$-5^2 + (2 \times -5) - 8 < 0$

$25 - 10 - 8 \leq 0$

$25 - 18 \leq 0$

$7 \leq 0$ INCORRECT

So, we have proved that $-4 \leq x \leq 2$.

128) The correct answer is D. Notice that the equation and the inequality both contain $x - 15$. So, we can substitute y for $x - 15$ in the inequality.

x − 15 > 0 and x − 15 = y

y > 0

129) The correct answer is A. You should use the FOIL method in this problem. Be very careful with the negative numbers when doing the multiplication.

$2(x + 2)(x − 3) =$

$2[(x \times x) + (x \times -3) + (2 \times x) + (2 \times -3)] =$

$2(x^2 + -3x + 2x + -6) =$

$2(x^2 − 3x + 2x − 6) =$

$2(x^2 − x − 6)$

Then multiply each term by the 2 at the front of the parentheses.

$2(x^2 − x − 6) =$

$2x^2 − 2x − 12$

130) The correct answer is B. Looking at this expression, we can see that each term contains x. We can also see that each term contains y. So, first factor out xy: $2xy − 6x^2y + 4x^2y^2 = xy(2 − 6x + 4xy)$. We can also see that all of the terms inside the parentheses are divisible by 2. So, let's factor out the 2 to get the other factor. To do this, we divide each term in the parentheses by 2: $xy(2 − 6x + 4xy) = 2xy(1 − 3x + 2xy)$

131) The correct answer is B. First, we need to calculate the shortage in the amount of houses actually built. If H represents the amount of houses that should be built and A represents the actual number of houses built, then the shortage is calculated as: $H − A$. The company has to pay P dollars per house for the shortage, so we calculate the total penalty by multiplying the shortage by the penalty per house:

$(H − A) \times P$

132) The correct answer is B. Step 1 – Apply the distributive property of multiplication by multiplying the first term in the first set of parentheses by all of the terms inside the second pair of parentheses. Then multiply the second term from the first set of parentheses by all of the terms inside the second set of parentheses.

$(5ab - 6a)(3ab^3 - 4b^2 - 3a) =$

$(5ab \times 3ab^3) + (5ab \times -4b^2) + (5ab \times -3a) + (-6a \times 3ab^3) + (-6a \times -4b^2) + (-6a \times -3a)$

Step 2 – Add up the individual products in order to solve the problem:

$(5ab \times 3ab^3) + (5ab \times -4b^2) + (5ab \times -3a) + (-6a \times 3ab^3) + (-6a \times -4b^2) + (-6a \times -3a) =$

$15a^2b^4 - 20ab^3 - 15a^2b - 18a^2b^3 + 24ab^2 + 18a^2$

133) The correct answer is A. To divide, invert the second fraction and then multiply as shown.

$$\frac{x}{5} \div \frac{9}{y} = \frac{x}{5} \times \frac{y}{9} = \frac{x \times y}{5 \times 9} = \frac{xy}{45}$$

134) The correct answer is D. Place the integers on one side of the inequality.

$-3x + 14 < 5$

$-3x + 14 - 14 < 5 - 14$

$-3x < -9$

Then get rid of the negative number. We need to reverse the way that the inequality sign points because we are dividing by a negative.

$-3x < -9$

$-3x \div -3 > -9 \div -3$ ("Less than" becomes "greater than" because we divide by a negative number.)

$x > 3$

3.15 is greater than 3, so it is the correct answer.

135) The correct answer is A.

FIRST: $(\boldsymbol{x} - 2y)(\boldsymbol{2x^2} - y) = x \times 2x^2 = 2x^3$

OUTSIDE: $(\boldsymbol{x} - 2y)(2x^2 - \boldsymbol{y}) = x \times -y = -xy$

INSIDE: $(x - \boldsymbol{2y})(\boldsymbol{2x^2} - y) = -2y \times 2x^2 = -4x^2y$

LAST: $(x - \boldsymbol{2y})(2x^2 - \boldsymbol{y}) = -2y \times -y = 2y^2$

SOLUTION: $2x^3 + -xy + -4x^2y + 2y^2 = 2x^3 - 4x^2y + 2y^2 - xy$

136) The correct answer is A. Put in the values of 4 for x and –3 for y and simplify.

$2x^2 + 5xy - y^2 =$

$(2 \times 4^2) + (5 \times 4 \times -3) - (-3^2) =$

$(2 \times 4 \times 4) + (5 \times 4 \times -3) - (-3 \times -3) =$

$(2 \times 16) + (20 \times -3) - (9) =$

$32 + (-60) - 9 =$

$32 - 60 - 9 =$

$32 - 69 = -37$

137) The correct answer is C.

$6 + 8(2\sqrt{x} + 4) = 62$

$6 - 6 + 8(2\sqrt{x} + 4) = 62 - 6$

$8(2\sqrt{x} + 4) = 56$

$16\sqrt{x} + 32 = 56$

$16\sqrt{x} + 32 - 32 = 56 - 32$

$16\sqrt{x} = 24$

$16\sqrt{x} \div 16 = 24 \div 16$

$\sqrt{x} = 24 \div 16$

$\sqrt{x} = \dfrac{24}{16}$

$\sqrt{x} = \dfrac{24 \div 8}{16 \div 8} = \dfrac{3}{2}$

138) The correct answer is D. $\sqrt{18} \times \sqrt{8} = \sqrt{18 \times 8} = \sqrt{144} = \sqrt{12 \times 12} = 12$

139) The correct answer is A. Perform the multiplication on the terms in the parentheses.

$2(3x - 1) = 4(x + 1) - 3$

$6x - 2 = (4x + 4) - 3$

Then simplify.

$6x - 2 = (4x + 4) - 3$

$6x - 2 = 4x + 1$

$6x - 2 - 1 = 4x + 1 - 1$

$6x - 3 = 4x$

Then isolate x to get your answer.

$6x - 3 = 4x$

$6x - 4x - 3 = 4x - 4x$

$2x - 3 = 0$

$2x - 3 + 3 = 0 + 3$

$2x = 3$

$2x \div 2 = 3 \div 2$

$x = {}^3/_2$

140) The correct answer is C. The first point on the graph lies at $x = 10$, so we can eliminate answer choices A and B. The point for the y coordinate that corresponds to $x = 10$ is 63 not 68, so we can eliminate answer choice D.

141) The correct answer is D. Isolate the whole numbers to one side of the equation first.

$20 - \frac{3x}{4} \geq 17$

$(20 - 20) - \frac{3x}{4} \geq 17 - 20$

$-\frac{3x}{4} \geq -3$

Then get rid of the fraction.

$-\frac{3x}{4} \geq -3$

$\left(4 \times -\frac{3x}{4}\right) \geq -3 \times 4$

$-3x \geq -12$

Then deal with the remaining whole numbers.

−3x ≥ −12

−3x ÷ −3 ≥ −12 ÷ −3

x ≤ 4

Remember to reverse the way the sign points when you divide by a negative number.

142) The correct answer is B. Substitute the values into the equation to solve. For $x = 2$ and $y = 3$:

10x + 3y = (10 × 2) + (3 × 3) = 20 + 9 = 29

143) The correct answer is B. The formula for perimeter is as follows: P = 2W + 2L. The patch is 12 yards by 10 yards, so we need 12 yards × 2 for the long sides patch and 10 yards × 2 for the shorter sides of the patch: (2 × 10) + (2 × 12) = 20 + 24 = 44

144) The correct answer is A. We start off with point B, which is represented by the coordinates (0, 2). The line is then shifted 5 units to the left and 4 units up. When we go to the left, we need to deduct the units, and when we go up we need to add units. So, do the operations on each of the coordinates in order to solve: 0 − 5 = −5 and 2 + 4 = 6, so our new coordinates are (−5, 6).

145) The correct answer is A. You need to use the distance formula: $d = \sqrt{(x_2 - x_1)^2 + (y_2 - y_1)^2}$
Put in the values provided, which were $(4\sqrt{7}, -2)$ and $(7\sqrt{7}, 4)$. Then multiply and simplify to solve.

$\sqrt{(x_2 - x_1)^2 + (y_2 - y_1)^2} =$

$\sqrt{(7\sqrt{7} - 4\sqrt{7})^2 + (4 - -2)^2} =$

$\sqrt{(3\sqrt{7})^2 + (6)^2} =$

$\sqrt{(9 \times 7) + 36} =$

$\sqrt{63 + 36} =$

$\sqrt{99} = \sqrt{9 \times 11} = 3\sqrt{11}$

146) The correct answer is B. The number of deserts is D and the number of main dishes is M. There are 4 family members, so both D and M are equal to 4.

(D × ?) + (M × $8) = $48

(4 × ?) + (4 × $8) = $48

(4 × ?) + $32 = $48

(4 × ?) + $32 − $32 = $48 − $32

4 × ? = $16

(4 × ?) ÷ 4 = $16 ÷ 4

? = $4

147) The correct answer is B. Substitute $x + 2$ for x in the original function to solve. So, $x^2 + 3x - 8$ becomes $(x+3)^2 + 3(x+3) - 8$

148) The correct answer is C. Negative numbers do not have square roots that are real numbers. So, we need to use an imaginary number to solve this problem.

149) The correct answer is B. Divide the capacity by the time in order to get the rate: 1200 gallons ÷ 75 minutes = 16 gallons per minute.

150) The correct answer is B. The two projects are being given different weights, so each project needs to have its own variable. Project X counts for 45% of the final grade, so the weighted value of project X is .45X. Project Y counts for 55%, so the weighted value of project Y is .55Y. The final grade is the total of the values for the two projects. So, we add to get our equation: .45X + .55Y

Solutions and Explanations for Practice Test Set 4 – Questions 241 to 320

151) The correct answer is D. Set up each part of the problem as an equation. The museum had twice as many visitors on Tuesday (T) as on Monday (M), so T = 2M. The number of visitors on Wednesday exceeded that of Tuesday by 20%, so W = 1.20 × T. Then express T in terms of M for Wednesday's visitors: W = 1.20 × T = 1.20 × 2M = 2.40M. Finally, add the amounts together for all three days:
M + 2M + 2.40M = 5.4M

152) The correct answer is C. Yesterday the train traveled $117^3/_4$ miles, and today it traveled $102^1/_6$ miles. To find the difference, we subtract these two amounts. Because the fraction on the first mixed number is greater than the fraction on the second mixed number, we can subtract the whole numbers and the fractions separately: $117^3/_4$ miles – $102^1/_6$ miles = ? Step 1 – Subtract the whole numbers: 117 – 102 = 15 miles. Step 2 – Perform the operation on the fractions by finding the lowest common denominator. $^3/_4$ miles – $^1/_6$ miles = ? In order to find the LCD, we would normally need to find the common factors first. Our denominators in this problem are 4 and 6. The factors of 4 are: 1 × 4 = 4; 2 × 2 = 4. The factors of 6 are: 1 × 6 = 6; 2 × 3 = 6. We do not have two factors in common, so we know that we need to find a new denominator which is greater than 6. In this problem, the LCD is 12 since 3 × 4 = 12 and 2 × 6 = 12. So, we express the fractions $^3/_4$ miles + $^1/_6$ miles in their LCD form: $^3/_4$ × $^3/_3$ = $^9/_{12}$ and $^1/_6$ × $^2/_2$ = $^2/_{12}$. Then subtract these two fractions: $^9/_{12}$ – $^2/_{12}$ = $^7/_{12}$. Step 3 – Combine the results from the two previous steps to solve the problem: $117^3/_4$ miles – $102^1/_6$ miles = $15^7/_{12}$ miles.

153) The correct answer is D. Sam is driving at 70 miles per hour, and at 10:30 am he is 140 miles from Farnam. Step 1 – We need to find out how far he will be from Farnam at 11:00 am, so we need to work out how far he will travel in 30 minutes. Step 2 – If Sam is traveling at 70 miles an hour, then he travels 35 minutes in half an hour: 70 miles in one hour × $^1/_2$ hour = 35 miles. Step 3 – If he was 140 miles from Farnam at 10:30 am, he will be 105 miles from Farnam at 11:00 am: 140 – 35 = 105 miles

154) The correct answer is C. The twelve students who failed the test represent one-third of the class. Since one-third of the students have failed, we can think of the class as being divided into three groups:

Group 1: The 12 students who failed; Group 2: 12 students who would have passed; Group 3: 12 more students who would have passed. So, the class consists of 36 students in total. In other words, we need to multiply by three to find the total number of students: 12 × 3 = 36

155) The correct answer is B. The problem tells us that sales this week were $600 and sales last week were $525. Step 1 – First, we need to find the difference in sales between the two weeks: $600 - $525 = $75 more in sales this week. Step 2 – Since each book is sold for $5, we divide this figure into the total in order to find out how many books were sold: $75 more sales ÷ $5 per book = 15 more books sold this week.

156) The correct answer is D. A percentage can always be expressed as a number with two decimal places. For example, 15% = 0.15 and 20% = 0.20. In our problem, 16% = 0.16. So D is correct.

157) The correct answer is B. Step 1 – First of all, you need to calculate the amount of the discount: $18 original price × 40% = $18 × 0.40 = $7.20 discount. Step 2 – Then deduct the amount of the discount from the original price to calculate the sales price of the item: $18 original price - $7.20 discount = $10.80 sales price.

158) The correct answer is B. If David answered 18 questions incorrectly on the exam and lost 36 points, and he then earned 25 extra credit points, his score was lowered by 11 points. Step 1 – To do the calculation, we need to take the points lost on the exam and add the extra credit points: –36 + 25 = –11. Step 2 – Since the question is asking how much the score was lowered, you need to give the amount as a positive number.

159) The correct answer is A. Step 1 – Convert the first fraction to the common denominator: 5/8 = (5 × 2)/(8 × 2) = 10/16. Step 2 – Subtract one increment from this to get your result: 10/16 – 1/16 = 9/16

160) The correct answer is B. Step 1 – Work out the cost for your usual supplier: 120 units × $172 = $20,640. Step 2 – Calculate the price for the third supplier: $19,000 + ($19,000 × .07) = $19,000 + $1,330

= $20,330. Step 3 – Compare to other deals to solve. The other deals are $20,640 and $20,500, so $20,330 is the best deal.

161) The correct answer is D. Step 1 – Determine the dollar value of the discount: $22.50 – $20 = $2.5. Step 2 – Divide the result from step 1 by the original price to get the percentage: $2.50 ÷ $22.50 = 0.1111 = 11.11%, which we round to 11%.

162) The correct answer is C. Step 1 – Calculate the amount of the tax increase: $480 × 7.5% = ? $480 original tax amount × 0.075 = $36 proposed increase in tax. Step 2 – Then add the increase to the original amount to get the amount of the tax after the proposed increase: $480 original tax + $36 increase in tax = $516 tax after increase

163) The correct answer is B. If there are 12 children and each one is supposed to receive 4 items, we can do the calculation as follows: 12 children × 4 items per child = 48 items required in total. Now subtract the total from the amount she already has in order to determine how many more she needs: 48 items required in total – 40 items available = 8 items still needed.

164) The correct answer is C. First of all, you have to find out how many students were absent on Tuesday. To find the number of absent students, you have to multiply the total number of students in the class by the percentage of the absence for Tuesday: 20 students in total × 5% = 1 student absent on Tuesday. Now calculate the absences for Wednesday in the same way: 20 students in total × 20% = 4 students absent on Wednesday. The problem is asking you how many more students were absent on Wednesday than Tuesday, so you need to subtract the two figures that you have just calculated.
4 students absent on Wednesday – 1 student absent on Tuesday = 3 students. So, 3 more students were absent on Wednesday.

165) The correct answer is B. The problem is asking you for the amount that the number of births per hospital in Johnson County for 2016 exceeded those for 1998. Step 1 – First we have to calculate the amount for 2016. In order to calculate this figure, you have to divide the total births by the number of

hospitals in each data set. For 2016, we have 240 total births and 15 hospitals in the data set: 240 ÷ 15 = 16 births per hospital for 2016. Step 2 – Now calculate the amount for 1998. In our problem, this amount is provided. We can see that there were 12 births per hospital in Johnson County in 1998. Step 3 – Now subtract the amounts for the two years to get your answer: 16 – 12 = 4 more births per hospital in 2016.

166) The correct answer is D. Step 1 – You need to multiply the number of miles that she is going to travel by the amount of time it takes her to travel one mile: 17 minutes for 1 mile × 5 miles to travel = 85 minutes needed. Step 2 – Now express the result in hours and minutes, remembering of course that an hour has 60 minutes: 85 minutes – 60 minutes = 25 minutes left. So, the answer is 1 hour and 25 minutes.

167) The correct answer is D. Sam's final grade for a class is based on his scores from a midterm test (M), a project (P), and a final exam (F), but the midterm test counts twice as much as the project, and the final exam counts twice as much as the midterm. Therefore, we have to count variable M twice. The value of the midterm is doubled and variable F is double of the midterm, so we have to count variable F 4 times. So, the equation is: P + 2M + 4F

168) The correct answer is D. The problem tells us that Bart rides at a rate of 12 miles per hour. We also know that he arrives in the town of Wilmington at 3:00 pm. The question is asking us how far Bart will be from Mount Pleasant at 5:00 pm. Step 1 – Calculate the time difference: 5:00 pm – 3:00 pm = 2 hours difference. Step 2 – Calculate the distance traveled: 12 miles per hour × 2 hours = 24 miles traveled. Step 3 – Calculate the distance left. The town of Mount Pleasant is 50 miles from Wilmington: 50 miles to travel – 24 miles traveled = 26 miles left.

169) The correct answer is C. The ticket office sold 360 more tickets on Friday than it did on Saturday. The office sold 2570 tickets in total during Friday and Saturday. Step 1 – Subtract the extra tickets sold on Friday: 2570 – 360 = 2210. Step 2 – Allocate the figure from step 1 to each day: 2210 ÷ 2 = 1105. Step 3 – Calculate Friday's amount by adding back in the excess: 1105 + 360 = 1465.

170) The correct answer is C. Step 1 – Calculate the beginning height in inches. Remember that there are 12 inches in a foot: 5 feet × 12 inches per foot = 60 inches in height. Step 2 – Calculate the increase in height: 60 inches × 10% = 6 inches. Step 3 – Calculate the new height by adding the increase to the number at the beginning: 5 feet + 6 inches = 5 feet 6 inches.

171) The correct answer is D. Step 1 – Calculate the amount of money spent on the original purchase of the jeans: 2 × $22.98 = $45.96. Step 2 – Calculate the value of the items acquired in the exchange, which in this case, is the value of the sweaters: 3 × $15.50 = $46.50. Step 3 – Calculate the difference between the value of the items acquired and the amount of money originally spent. Value of the items acquired: 3 × $15.50 = $46.50. Amount of money originally spent: 2 × $22.98 = $45.96. Calculate the difference:

(3 × $15.50) – (2 × $22.98)

172) The correct answer is D. We know that we have to round to the nearest hundredth. The hundredth decimal place is the number 2 positions to the right of the decimal. For example, .01 is 1 one hundredth. In our question, the first jump of 3.246 is rounded up to 3.25. The second jump of 3.331 is rounded down to 3.33. The third jump of 3.328 is rounded up to 3.33. Then add these three figures together to get your answer: 3.25 + 3.33 + 3.33 = 9.91

173) The correct answer is D. You have to find the relationship between the number given in each row in the left column and the corresponding number in the right column. "9:50 am to 10:36 am" represents a journey time of 46 minutes. 11:15 to 12:01 is also 46 minutes, and so on. If we go 46 minutes back from 5:51 pm, we get 5:05 pm for our answer.

174) The correct answer is B. He owns 26 yachts and needs 6 feet 10 inches of rope for each one. Convert the feet and inches measurement to inches: 6 feet 10 inches = (6 × 12) + 10 inches = 72 + 10 = 82 inches. Then multiply buy the number of items: 26 × 82 = 2132 inches of rope needed. Then convert back to feet and inches: 2132 inches ÷ 12 = 177 feet 8 inches.

175) The correct answer is C. Step 1 – You can simplify the first fraction because both the numerator and denominator are divisible by 3: $^3/_6 \div {}^3/_3 = {}^1/_2$. Step 2 – Then divide the denominator of the second fraction ($^x/_{14}$) by the denominator of the simplified fraction ($^1/_2$) from above: $14 \div 2 = 7$. Step 3 – Now, multiply the number from step 2 by the numerator of the fraction we calculated in step 1 in order to get your result: $1 \times 7 = 7$. You can check your answer as follows: $^3/_6 = {}^7/_{14}$; $^3/_6 \div {}^3/_3 = {}^1/_2$; $^7/_{14} \div {}^7/_7 = {}^1/_2$

176) The correct answer is D. This problem is asking for the ratio of non-faulty mp3 players to the quantity of faulty mp3 players. Therefore, you must put the quantity of non-faulty mp3 players before the colon in the ratio. In this problem, 1% of the players are faulty. 1% × 100 = 1 faulty player in every 100 players. 100 − 1 = 99 non-faulty players. So, the ratio is 99:1. As explained previously, the number before the colon and the number after the colon can be added together to get the total quantity.

177) The correct answer is A.

Factor: $x^2 + 4x + 3 > 0$

$(x + 1)(x + 3) > 0$

Then solve each parenthetical for zero:

$(x + 1) = 0$

$-1 + 1 = 0$

$x = -1$

$(x + 3) = 0$

$-3 + 3 = 0$

$x = -3$

So, $x < -3$ or $x > -1$

Now check. Use 0 to check to for $x > -1$. Since $0 > -1$ is correct, our proof for this should also be correct.

$x^2 + 4x + 3 > 0$

$0 + 0 + 3 > 0$

$3 > 0$ CORRECT

Use –2 to check for x < –3. Since –2 < –3 is incorrect, our proof should also be incorrect.

$x^2 + 4x + 3 > 0$

$-2^2 + (4 \times -2) + 3 > 0$

$4 - 8 + 3 > 0$

$-4 + 3 > 0$

$-1 > 0$ INCORRECT

Therefore, we have checked that x < –3 or x > –1

178) The correct answer is D. The most striking relationship on the graph is the line for ages 65 and over, which clearly shows a negative relationship between exercising outdoors and the number of days of rain per month. You will recall that a negative relationship exists when an increase in one variable causes a decrease in the other variable. So, we can conclude that people aged 65 and over seem less inclined to exercise outdoors when there is more rain.

179) The correct answer is C.

FIRST: $(\bm{x} - 9y)(\bm{x} - 9y) = x \times x = x^2$

OUTSIDE: $(\bm{x} - 9y)(x - \bm{9y}) = x \times -9y = -9xy$

INSIDE: $(x - \bm{9y})(\bm{x} - 9y) = -9y \times x = -9xy$

LAST: $(x - \bm{9y})(x - \bm{9y}) = -9y \times -9y = 81y^2$

SOLUTION: $x^2 - 18xy + 81y^2$

180) The correct answer is B. Deal with the whole numbers first.

$6 + \frac{x}{4} \geq 22$

$6 - 6 + \frac{x}{4} \geq 22 - 6$

$\frac{x}{4} \geq 16$

Then eliminate the fraction.

$\frac{x}{4} \geq 16$

$$4 \times \frac{x}{4} \geq 16 \times 4$$

$$x \geq 64$$

181) The correct answer is A. Perform long division of the polynomial.

```
            x + 3
       ┌─────────────
x − 4 )  x² − x − 12
         x² − 4x
         ─────────
              3x − 12
              3x − 12
              ───────
                    0
```

182) The correct answer is A. Factor out xy: $18xy - 24x^2y - 48y^2x^2 = xy(18 - 24x - 48xy)$

Then, factor out the common factor of 6: $xy(18 - 24x - 48xy) = 6xy(3 - 4x - 8xy)$

183) The correct answer is C. Multiply the integers and add the exponents on the variables:

$\sqrt{15x^3} \times \sqrt{8x^2} =$

$\sqrt{15x^3 \times 8x^2} =$

$\sqrt{15 \times 8 \times x^3 \times x^2} =$

$\sqrt{120x^5} = \sqrt{2 \times 2 \times x^2 \times x^2 \times x \times 30} = 2x^2\sqrt{30x}$

184) The correct answer is B. We know from the second equation that y is equal to x + 7. So put x + 7 into the first equation for the value of y to solve.

−3x − 1 = y

−3x − 1 = x + 7

−3x − 1 + 1 = x + 7 + 1

−3x − x = x − x + 8

−4x = 8

−4x ÷ −4 = 8 ÷ −4

x = −2

Now we know that the value of x is –2, so we can put that into the equation to solve for y.

–3x – 1 = y

(–3 × –2) – 1 = y

6 – 1 = y

y = 5

185) The correct answer is D. Any negative exponent is equal to 1 divided by the variable. Accordingly, $x^{-4} = 1 \div x^4$

186) The correct answer is C. Deal with the integers that are outside the parentheses first. Then remove the radical to solve.

$5(4\sqrt{x} - 8) = 40$

$20\sqrt{x} - 40 = 40$

$20\sqrt{x} - 40 + 40 = 40 + 40$

$20\sqrt{x} = 80$

$20\sqrt{x} \div 20 = 80 \div 20$

$\sqrt{x} = 4$

$\sqrt{x}^2 = 4^2$

$x = 16$

187) The correct answer is B. We can see that when $x = 80$, $y = 60$. So, when $x = 160$, $y = 120$. Alternatively, if you prefer, you can determine that the line represents the function: $f(x) = x \times 0.75$. Then substitute 160 for x: $x \times 0.75 = 160 \times 0.75 = 120$

188) The correct answer is C. Perform the operation inside the absolute value signs then make the result negative since there is a negative sign in front of the absolute value: – | 5 – 8| = – | –3| = – |3| = –3

189) The correct answer is C.

Here is the solution for y intercept:

$5x^2 + 4y^2 = 120$

$5(0)^2 + 4y^2 = 120$

$0 + 4y^2 = 120$

$4y^2 = 120$

$4y^2 \div 4 = 120 \div 4$

$y^2 = 30$

$y = \sqrt{30}$

So, the y intercept is $(0, \sqrt{30})$

Here is the solution for x intercept:

$5x^2 + 4y^2 = 120$

$5x^2 + 4(0)^2 = 120$

$5x^2 + 0 = 120$

$5x^2 = 120$

$5x^2 \div 5 = 120 \div 5$

$x^2 = \sqrt{24}$

So the x intercept is $(\sqrt{24}, 0)$

190) The correct answer is B. Use the slope-intercept formula to calculate the slope: $y = mx + b$, where m is the slope and b is the y intercept. In our question, $x = 4$ and $y = 15$. The line crosses the y axis at 3, so put the values into the formula.

$y = mx + b$

$15 = m4 + 3$

$15 - 3 = m4 + 3 - 3$

$12 = m4$

$12 \div 4 = m$

$3 = m$

191) The correct answer is C. Substitute the values into the equation to solve. For $x = 2$ and $y = 4$,

$5x + 6y = (5 \times 2) + (6 \times 4) = 10 + 24 = 34$.

192) The correct answer is D. The slopes of perpendicular lines are negative reciprocals of each other. The equation for line K is in the slope-intercept form: $y = 5x + 0$, so the slope of line K is 5. To find the reciprocal of line K, you need to invert the whole number (5) to make a fraction. So, 5 becomes $\frac{1}{5}$. You then need to make this a negative number, so $\frac{1}{5}$ becomes $-\frac{1}{5}$. Line L has a y intercept of 0 because the facts of the question state that line L passes through (0, 0). Using the slope intercept formula for line L with a slope of $-\frac{1}{5}$ and a y intercept of 0, we get our answer: $y = -\frac{1}{5}x + 0$. Removing the zero, we get $y = -\frac{1}{5}x$.

193) The correct answer is C. Let's say the number widgets is represented by D and the number whatsits is represented by H. Your equation is: $(D \times \$2) + (H \times \$25) = \$85$. We know that the number of whatsits is 3, so put that in the equation and solve for the number of widgets.

$(D \times \$2) + (H \times \$25) = \$85$

$(D \times \$2) + (3 \times \$25) = \$85$

$(D \times \$2) + \$75 = \$85$

$(D \times \$2) + 75 - 75 = \$85 - \$75$

$(D \times \$2) = \$10$

$\$2D = \$10$

$\$2D \div 2 = \$10 \div 2$

$D = 5$

194) The correct answer is B. Remember that $\sqrt{x} = x^{\frac{1}{2}}$, so $\sqrt{3} = 3^{\frac{1}{2}}$

195) The correct answer is A. Miles per hour (MPH) is calculated as follows: miles ÷ hours = MPH.

So, if we have the MPH and the miles traveled, we need to change the above equation in order to calculate the hours.

miles ÷ hours = MPH

miles ÷ hours × hours = MPH × hours

miles = MPH × hours

miles ÷ MPH = (MPH × hours) ÷ MPH

miles ÷ MPH = hours

In other words, we divide the number of miles by the miles per hour to get the time for each part of the event. So, for the first part of the event, the hours are calculated as follows: 80 ÷ 5. For the second part of the event, we take the remaining mileage and divide by the unknown variable: 20 ÷ x. Since the event is divided into two parts, these two results added together equal the total time.

Total time = [(80 ÷ 5) + (20 ÷ x)]

The total amount of miles for the event is then divided by the total time to get the average miles per hour for the entire event. We have a 100 mile endurance event, so the result is: 100 ÷ [(80 ÷ 5) + (20 ÷ x)]

196) The correct answer is C. If she uses 12 cups of sugar, she is using 6 times the basic amount of 2 cups. (2 cups × 6 = 12 cups). So, to keep things in proportion, we also need to multiply the basic amount of one-third cup of butter by six: $^1/_3$ × 6 = 2 cups of butter

197) The correct answer is C. We know that she traveled 150 miles before the repair. Miles traveled before needing the repair: 60 MPH × 2.5 hours = 150 miles traveled. If the journey is 240 miles in total, she has 90 miles remaining after the car is repaired: 240 – 150 = 90. If she then travels at 75 miles an hour for 90 miles, the time she spends is: 90 ÷ 75 = 1.2 hours. There are 60 minutes in an hour, so 1.2 hours is 1 hour and 12 minutes because 60 minutes × 0.20 = 12 minutes. The time spent traveling after the repair is 1 hour and 12 minutes. Now add together all of the times to get your answer: Time spent before needing the repair: 2.5 hours = 2 hours and 30 minutes; Time spent waiting for the repair: 2 hours; The time spent traveling after the repair: 1 hour and 12 minutes; Total time: 5 hours and 42 minutes. If she left home at 6:00 am, she will arrive in Denver at 11:42 am.

198) The correct answer is C. If the amount earned from selling jackets was one-third that of selling jeans, the ratio of jacket to jean sales was 1 to 3. So, we need to divide the total sales of $4,000 into $1,000 for jackets and $3,000 for jeans. We can then solve as follows:

$3,000 in jeans sales ÷ $20 per pair = 150 pairs sold

199) The correct answer is D. Divide each side of the equation by 3. Then subtract 5 from both sides of the equation as shown below.

$18 = 3(x + 5)$

$18 \div 3 = [3(x + 5)] \div 3$

$6 = x + 5$

$6 - 5 = x + 5 - 5$

$1 = x$

200) The correct answer is A. The tank has a 500 gallon capacity and it is being filled at a rate of 3.5 gallons per minute, so we divide to get the time: $500 \div 3.5 = 142.85$ minutes $\approx$ 2 hours and 23 minutes.

Solutions and Explanations for Practice Test Set 5 – Questions 321 to 400

201) The correct answer is D. Step 1 – Convert into minutes the amount of time required to make one cap: 4 hours and 10 minutes = (4 × 60) + 10 = 240 + 10 = 250 minutes needed to make one cap. Step 2 – Multiply by the total output: 250 minutes × 12 caps = 3000 minutes. Step 3 – Convert the total amount of minutes back to hours and minutes: 3000 minutes ÷ 60 = 50 hours.

202) The correct answer is D. Add the feet above ground to the feet below ground to get the total distance: 525 + 95 = 620 feet.

203) The correct answer is C. Step 1 – Add the items together to get the total amount of items available: 13 + 22 + 25 = 60 balloons in total. Step 2 – Divide the amount of items available by the number of people: 60 ÷ 12 = 5.

204) The correct answer is B. Step 1 – Determine the value of the discount by multiplying the normal price by the percentage discount: $90 × 15% = $13.50 discount. Step 2 – Subtract the value of the discount from the normal price to get the new price: $90 – $13.50 = $76.50.

205) The correct answer is C. Step 1 – You can express the fractions as decimals for the sake of simplicity: 10½ = 10.50; 7¾ = 7.75. Step 2 – Then subtract to find the increase: 10.50 – 7.75 = 2.75. Step 3 – Then convert back to a mixed number: 2.75 = 2¾

206) The correct answer is A. After her raise, she earns $184 per week. She continues to work 23 hours per week. Step 1 – Determine the new hourly rate: $184 ÷ 23 hours = $8 per hour. Step 2 – Determine the change in the hourly rate: $8 - $7.50 = 50 cents per hour.

207) The correct answer is A. Step 1 – Determine the distance traveled. If he is traveling 70 miles an hour, he will have traveled 70 miles after one hour has passed. Step 2 – Determine the distance from the towns listed on the sign, considering that he has traveled for one hour. Washington: 140 – 70 = 70 miles from Washington; Yorkville: 105 – 70 = 35 miles from Yorkville; Zorster: 210 – 70 = 140 miles from

Zorster. Step 3 – Compare the above figures to your answer choices to get your result. After an hour, he is 70 miles from Washington, so A is correct.

208) The correct answer is D. Step 1 – Subtract the extra cars in the morning from the total: 300 – 114 = 186. Step 2 – Allocate the result from Step 1 into its respective parts. We are dividing the day into two parts: morning and afternoon. There were 186 cars in total without the excess, so divide this into two parts: 186 ÷ 2 = 93. Step 3 – Determine the amount for the larger part. There were 114 more cars in the morning, so add this back in: 93 + 114 = 207 cars in the morning.

209) The correct answer is B. Step 1 – Think about the value of the four pairs of socks she is getting in the exchange. These socks cost 50 cents more each than the pairs she has already bought. So, we can express the difference in value of those four pairs of socks as: 4 × ($3 - $2.50). Step 2 – Take into account the value of the extra pair of socks. She paid $2.50 for a fifth pair of socks, but she is only getting four pairs back on the exchange, so she is owed money back for that part of the purchase. Therefore, we can calculate the refund owing as $2.50 – 4($3 - $2.50)

210) The correct answer is A. The line in any fraction can be treated as the division symbol. Accordingly, we can divide by the denominator, which is 100 in this case.

$$\frac{35 \times 90}{100} = (35 \times 90) \div 100$$

211) The correct answer is D. A 12 pound container of item B costs $48. Therefore, it costs $4 per pound ($48 ÷ 12 pounds = $4 per pound). Item C costs 20% more per pound than item B. In other words, Item C costs 80 cents more ($4 × 20% = 0.80). So, the cost per pound of item C is $4.80.

212) The correct answer is B. The cost of the photography course is $20 per week plus a $5 fee per week for review of photographs and administration. So, the course costs $25 per week. To get the total cost we need to multiply by the number of weeks, which is represented by variable W. Therefore, the total cost of the course and fees for W weeks is $25 × W = $25W.

213) The correct answer is A. Remember that when two fractions have the same numerator, the fraction with the smaller number in the denominator is the larger fraction. So, $-1/4$ is less than $1/8$, $1/8$ is less than $1/6$, and $1/6$ is less than 1.

214) The correct answer is C. This question asks you to interpret a graph in order to determine the price per unit of an item. To solve the problem, look at the graph and then divide the total sales in dollars by the total quantity sold in order to get the price per unit. For ten hamburgers, the total price is $85, so each hamburger sells for $8.50: $85 total sales in dollars ÷ 10 hamburgers sold = $8.50 each. The cost of shakes is represented by: $c = \frac{9}{4}s \cdot \frac{9}{4} = (9 \div 4)s = 2.25s$, so each shake costs $2.25. So, the difference between the cost of one hamburger and the cost of one shake is $8.50 – $2.25 = $6.25

215) The correct answer is D. The tenths place is the first place to the right of the decimal, so 12.86749 rounded to the nearest tenth is 12.9. We have to round up because the number in the hundredths place (7) is 5 or greater.

216) The correct answer is B. Treat the line in the fraction as the division symbol: $2/5$ = 2 ÷ 5 = 0.40

217) The correct answer is C. Step 1 – Take the total number of employees and divide this by 5: 250 ÷ 5 = 50. Step 2 – The question asks how many questionnaires have not been completed and returned, so subtract to find the amount in the 'not returned' subset: 5 – 4 = 1. Step 3 – Multiply the result from step 2 by the result from step 1 to solve: 50 × 1 = 50

218) The correct answer is D. Step 1 – Determine the total for sales in December: $20 × 55 = $1,100. Step 2 – Determine the total sales for January: $12 × 20 = $240. Step 3 – Add these two amounts to solve: $1,100 + $240 = $1,340

219) The correct answer is C. In this problem, the fraction on the second number is larger than the fraction on the first number, so we need to covert the first fraction before we start our calculation. Step 1 – Convert $28^3/_{10}$ for subtraction: $28^3/_{10} = 27^3/_{10} + 1 = 27^3/_{10} + {^{10}/_{10}} = 27^{13}/_{10}$. Step 2 – Subtract the whole numbers. You have spent $7^9/_{10}$ hours on the job so far, so subtract the 7 hours: 27 – 7 = 20.

Step 3 – Subtract the fractions: 13/10 – 9/10 = 4/10. Step 4 – Simplify the fraction from step 3 – 4/10 = (4 ÷ 2)/(10 ÷ 2) = 2/5. Step 4 – Combine the results from step 2 and step 4 to get your new mixed number to solve the problem: 20 + 2/5 = 20²/₅

220) The correct answer is C. Step 1 – Take the 147 parts of blue slate chippings for this order and divide by the 3 parts stated in the original ratio: 147 ÷ 3 = 49. Step 2 – Multiply the result from step 1 by the 2 parts of white gravel stated in the original ratio to get your answer: 49 × 2 = 98

221) The correct answer is C. The distance between point B and point C is 1.2. Point B is at 0.35, so point C is either 0.35 – 1.2 = –0.85 or 0.35 + 1.2 = 1.55.

222) The correct answer is B. 15.845 + 8.21 = 24.055. Rounding to the nearest integer, we remove the decimals to get 24.

223) The correct answer is C.

$(5x - 2)(3x^2 + 5x - 8) =$

$(5x \times 3x^2) + (5x \times 5x) + (5x \times -8) + (-2 \times 3x^2) + (-2 \times 5x) + (-2 \times -8) =$

$15x^3 + 25x^2 - 40x - 6x^2 - 10x + 16 =$

$15x^3 + 25x^2 - 6x^2 - 40x - 10x + 16 =$

$15x^3 + 19x^2 - 50x + 16$

224) The correct answer is A. You can subtract the second equation from the first equation as the first step in solving the problem. Look at the term containing x in the second equation. $8x$ is in the second equation. In order to eliminate the term containing x, we need to multiply the first equation by 8.

$x + 5y = 24$

$(x \times 8) + (5y \times 8) = 24 \times 8$

$8x + 40y = 192$

Now subtract.

$$8x + 40y = 192$$
$$-(8x + 2y = 40)$$
$$38y = 152$$

Then solve for y.

$$38y = 152$$

$$38y \div 38 = 152 \div 38$$

$$y = 4$$

Now put the value for y into the first equation and solve for x.

$$x + 5y = 24$$

$$x + (5 \times 4) = 24$$

$$x + 20 = 24$$

$$x = 4$$

$x = 4$ and $y = 4$, so the answer is (4, 4).

225) The correct answer is C. Find the lowest common denominator. Then add the numerators and simplify.

$$\frac{2}{10x} + \frac{3}{12x^2} =$$

$$\left(\frac{2 \times 6x}{10x \times 6x}\right) + \left(\frac{3 \times 5}{12x^2 \times 5}\right) =$$

$$\frac{12x}{60x^2} + \frac{15}{60x^2} = \frac{12x + 15}{60x^2} =$$

$$\frac{3(4x + 5)}{3 \times 20x^2} = \frac{\cancel{3}(4x + 5)}{\cancel{3} \times 20x^2} = \frac{4x + 5}{20x^2}$$

226) The correct answer is B. Find a perfect square for one of the factors for each radical. Then factor the integers inside each of the square root signs.

$$\sqrt{50} + 4\sqrt{32} + 7\sqrt{2} =$$

$$\sqrt{25 \times 2} + 4\sqrt{16 \times 2} + 7\sqrt{2} =$$

$5\sqrt{2} + (4 \times 4)\sqrt{2} + 7\sqrt{2} =$

$5\sqrt{2} + 16\sqrt{2} + 7\sqrt{2} = 28\sqrt{2}$

227) The correct answer is C. First perform the division on the integers: 10 ÷ 2 = 5

Then do the division on the other variables.

$a^2 \div a = a$

$b^3 \div b^2 = b$

$c \div c^2 = \dfrac{1}{c}$

Then multiply these results to get the solution.

$5 \times a \times b \times \dfrac{1}{c} = \dfrac{5ab}{c} = 5ab \div c$

228) The correct answer is B. Find the lowest common denominator.

$\dfrac{\sqrt{48}}{3} + \dfrac{5\sqrt{5}}{6} = \left(\dfrac{\sqrt{48}}{3} \times \dfrac{2}{2}\right) + \dfrac{5\sqrt{5}}{6} = \dfrac{2\sqrt{48}}{6} + \dfrac{5\sqrt{5}}{6}$

Then simplify, if possible: $\dfrac{2\sqrt{48}}{6} + \dfrac{5\sqrt{5}}{6} = \dfrac{2\sqrt{(4 \times 4) \times 3}}{6} + \dfrac{5\sqrt{5}}{6} = \dfrac{(2 \times 4)\sqrt{3}+5\sqrt{5}}{6} = \dfrac{8\sqrt{3}+5\sqrt{5}}{6}$

229) The correct answer is B. Substitute 1 for x: $\dfrac{x-3}{2-x} = \dfrac{1-3}{2-1} = (1 - 3) \div (2 - 1) = -2 \div 1 = -2$

230) The correct answer is D. Multiply the amounts inside the radical sign, but leave the cube root as it is: $\sqrt[3]{5} \times \sqrt[3]{7} = \sqrt[3]{35}$

231) The correct answer is D. Simplify the numerator and multiply the radicals in the denominator using the FOIL method. Then simplify the denominator.

$\dfrac{1}{\sqrt{x} - \sqrt{y}} \times \dfrac{\sqrt{x}+\sqrt{y}}{\sqrt{x}+\sqrt{y}} = \dfrac{\sqrt{x}+\sqrt{y}}{\sqrt{x}^2 + \sqrt{xy} - \sqrt{xy} - \sqrt{y}^2} = \dfrac{\sqrt{x}+\sqrt{y}}{\sqrt{x}^2 - \sqrt{y}^2} = \dfrac{\sqrt{x}+\sqrt{y}}{x-y}$

232) The correct answer is D. Factor each of the parentheticals in the expression: $(3x + 3y)(5a + 5b) = 3(x + y) \times 5(a + b)$. We know that $x + y = 5$ and $a + b = 4$, so we can substitute the values for each of the parentheticals: $3(x + y) \times 5(a + b) = 3(5) \times 5(4) = 15 \times 20 = 300$

233) The correct answer is D.

Step 1 – Factor the equation.

$x^2 + 6x + 8 = 0$

$(x + 2)(x + 4) = 0$

Step 2 – Now substitute 0 for x in the first pair of parentheses.

$(0 + 2)(x + 4) = 0$

$2(x + 4) = 0$

$2x + 8 = 0$

$2x + 8 - 8 = 0 - 8$

$2x = -8$

$2x \div 2 = -8 \div 2$

$x = -4$

Step 3 – Then substitute 0 for x in the second pair of parentheses.

$(x + 2)(x + 4) = 0$

$(x + 2)(0 + 4) = 0$

$(x + 2)4 = 0$

$4x + 8 = 0$

$4x + 8 - 8 = 0 - 8$

$4x = -8$

$4x \div 4 = -8 \div 4$

$x = -2$

234) The correct answer is C. The line in a fraction is the same as the division symbol. For example, $a/b = a \div b$. In the same way, $3/xy = 3 \div (xy)$.

235) The correct answer is D. Get the integers to one side of the equation first of all.

$\frac{1}{5}x + 3 = 5$

$\frac{1}{5}x + 3 - 3 = 5 - 3$

$\frac{1}{5}x = 2$

Then multiply to eliminate the fraction and solve the problem.

$\frac{1}{5}x \times 5 = 2 \times 5$

$x = 10$

236) The correct answer is C.

Factor: $x^2 - 12x + 35 < 0$

$(x - 7)(x - 5) < 0$

Then solve each parenthetical for zero:

$(x - 7) = 0$

$7 - 7 = 0$

$x = 7$

$(x - 5) = 0$

$5 - 5 = 0$

$x = 5$

So, $5 < x < 7$

Now check. Use 6 to check to for x < 7. Since 6 < 7 is correct, our proof for this should also be correct.

$x^2 - 12x + 35 < 0$

$6^2 - (12 \times 6) + 35 < 0$

$36 - 72 + 35 < 0$

$-36 + 35 < 0$

$-1 < 0$ CORRECT

Use 4 to check for x > 5, which is the same as 5 < x. Since 4 > 5 is incorrect, our proof for this should be incorrect.

$x^2 - 12x + 35 < 0$

$4^2 - (12 \times 4) + 35 < 0$

$16 - 48 + 35 < 0$

$-32 + 35 < 0$

$3 < 0$ INCORRECT

So, we have proved that 5 < x < 7.

237) The correct answer is C. Each term contains the variables x and y. So, factor out xy as shown: $2xy - 8x^2y + 6y^2x^2 = xy(2 - 8x + 6xy)$. Then, factor out any whole numbers. All of the terms inside the parentheses are divisible by 2, so factor out 2: $xy(2 - 8x + 6xy) = 2xy(1 - 4x + 3xy)$

238) The correct answer is A. The problem tells us that A is 3 times B, and B is 3 more than 6 times C. So, we need to create equations based on this information.

B is 3 more than 6 times C: B = 6C + 3

A is 3 times B: A = 3B

Since B = 6C + 3, we can substitute 6C + 3 for B in the second equation as follows:

A = 3B

A = 3(6C + 3)

A = 18C + 9

So, A is 9 more than 18 times C.

239) The correct answer is B. Perform the operation inside the absolute value signs: 6 – 13 = –7.

The absolute value of –7 is 7.

240) The correct answer is D. Our points are (5, 7) and (11, –3) so use the midpoint formula.

$(x_1 + x_2) \div 2$, $(y_1 + y_2) \div 2$

(5 + 11) ÷ 2 = midpoint x, (7 – 3) ÷ 2 = midpoint y

16 ÷ 2 = midpoint x, 4 ÷ 2 = midpoint y

8 = midpoint x, 2 = midpoint y

241) The correct answer is C. In order to find the value of a variable inside a square root sign, you need to square each side of the equation.

$\sqrt{9z + 18} = 9$

$\sqrt{9z + 18}^2 = 9^2$

$9z + 18 = 81$

$9z + 18 - 18 = 81 - 18$

$9z = 63$

$9z \div 9 = 63 \div 9$

$z = 7$

242) The correct answer is C. First you need to get rid of the fraction. To eliminate the fraction, multiply each side of the equation by the denominator of the fraction.

$z = \dfrac{x}{1 - y}$

$z \times (1 - y) = \dfrac{x}{1 - y} \times (1 - y)$

$z(1 - y) = x$

Then isolate y to solve.

$z(1 - y) \div z = x \div z$

$1 - y = x \div z$

$1 - 1 - y = (x \div z) - 1$

$-y = (x \div z) - 1$

$-y \times -1 = [(x \div z) - 1] \times -1$

$y = -\dfrac{x}{z} + 1$

243) The correct answer is D. Multiply the radical in front of the parentheses by each radical inside the parentheses. Then simplify further if possible.

$\sqrt{6} \cdot (\sqrt{40} + \sqrt{6}) =$

$(\sqrt{6} \times \sqrt{40}) + (\sqrt{6} \times \sqrt{6}) =$

$\sqrt{240} + 6 = \sqrt{16 \times 15} + 6 = 4\sqrt{15} + 6$

244) The correct answer is C. When you have fractions as exponents, the denominator of the faction is placed in front of the radical sign. The numerators become the new exponents as show below:

$a^{1/2} b^{1/4} c^{3/4} = \sqrt{a} \times \sqrt[4]{b} \times \sqrt[4]{c^3}$

245) The correct answer is A. If the base is the same, and you need to divide, you subtract the exponents: $ab^8 \div ab^2 = ab^{8-2} = ab^6$

246) The correct answer is C. He is using 14 ounces of plaster powder, so divide that by the basic amount of plaster of 4 ounces, stated in the instructions. $14 \div 4 = 3.5$. Then multiply this result by the basic amount of water of 3 ounces, stated in the instructions: $3 \times 3.5 = 10.5$

247) The correct answer is C. The y coordinate where $x = 10$ is $y = 65$. So, the graph represents the function $f(x) = x \times 6.50$. In other words, Item A sells for $6.50 a pound. The equation $C = p \times (7 \div 2)$ is equal to $C = 3.50p$ because $7 \div 2 = 3.5$. So, Item B sells for $3.50 per pound. Therefore, Item B costs $3 less per pound than Item A.

248) The correct answer is D. Find the lowest common denominator.

$\dfrac{1}{a+1} + \dfrac{1}{a} =$

$\left(\dfrac{1}{a+1} \times \dfrac{a}{a}\right) + \left(\dfrac{1}{a} \times \dfrac{a+1}{a+1}\right) =$

$\dfrac{a}{a^2+a} + \dfrac{a+1}{a^2+a}$

Then simplify, if possible

$$\frac{a}{a^2 + a} + \frac{a + 1}{a^2 + a} =$$

$$\frac{a + a + 1}{a^2 + a} = \frac{2a + 1}{a^2 + a}$$

249) The correct answer is D. Treat the main fraction as the division sign.

$$\frac{5x}{1/xy} = 5x \div \frac{1}{xy}$$

Then invert the second fraction and multiply as usual.

$$5x \div \frac{1}{xy} = 5x \times \frac{xy}{1} = 5x \times xy = 5x^2 y$$

250) The correct answer is C. Step 1 – Convert the mixed number to a decimal: $1^1/_4$ = 1.25 hours.

Step 2 – Multiply the result from the previous step by the number of intervals: 1.25 × 7 = 8.75 hours.

Step 3 – Convert the decimal to minutes: 0.75 hour = 45 minutes. Step 4 – Express your answer in hours and minutes: 8 hours and 45 minutes

ANSWER KEY

1) D

2) D

3) C

4) B

5) A

6) D

7) C

8) A

9) B

10) C

11) B

12) D

13) B

14) C

15) A

16) A

17) B

18) D

19) C

20) D

21) A

22) C

23) A

24) D

25) D

26) A

27) B

28) A

29) B

30) B

31) D

32) B

33) C

34) C

35) D

36) A

37) B

38) D

39) C

40) C

41) D	63) D
42) A	64) C
43) D	65) A
44) B	66) B
45) D	67) A
46) C	68) D
47) B	69) C
48) D	70) D
49) A	71) B
50) A	72) B
51) B	73) B
52) B	74) A
53) A	75) A
54) A	76) A
55) D	77) B
56) A	78) C
57) C	79) B
58) D	80) D
59) D	81) D
60) C	82) D
61) C	83) C
62) B	84) B

85) C	107) D
86) A	108) B
87) A	109) D
88) C	110) D
89) D	111) C
90) D	112) D
91) C	113) A
92) C	114) B
93) A	115) D
94) B	116) C
95) D	117) C
96) C	118) B
97) D	119) D
98) A	120) B
99) B	121) D
100) A	122) B
101) C	123) A
102) C	124) D
103) A	125) A
104) C	126) C
105) D	127) D
106) A	128) D

129) A	151) D
130) B	152) C
131) B	153) D
132) B	154) C
133) A	155) B
134) D	156) D
135) A	157) B
136) A	158) B
137) C	159) A
138) D	160) B
139) A	161) D
140) C	162) C
141) D	163) B
142) B	164) C
143) B	165) B
144) A	166) D
145) A	167) D
146) B	168) D
147) B	169) C
148) C	170) C
149) B	171) D
150) B	172) D

173) D	195) A
174) B	196) C
175) C	197) C
176) D	198) C
177) A	199) D
178) D	200) A
179) C	201) D
180) B	202) D
181) A	203) C
182) A	204) B
183) C	205) C
184) B	206) A
185) D	207) A
186) C	208) D
187) B	209) B
188) C	210) A
189) C	211) D
190) B	212) B
191) C	213) A
192) D	214) C
193) C	215) D
194) B	216) B

217) C

218) D

219) C

220) C

221) C

222) B

223) C

224) A

225) C

226) B

227) C

228) B

229) B

230) D

231) D

232) D

233) D

234) C

235) D

236) C

237) C

238) A

239) B

240) D

241) C

242) C

243) D

244) C

245) A

246) C

247) C

248) D

249) D

250) C

www.ingramcontent.com/pod-product-compliance
Lightning Source LLC
Chambersburg PA
CBHW060424010526
44118CB00017B/2347